THE OASIS THIS TIME

LIVING AND DYING
WITH WATER IN THE WEST

Praise for *The Oasis This Time*

"Rebecca Lawton's powerful and poetic *The Oasis This Time* celebrates water as a precious natural resource. The collection is as diverse as it is illuminating. Each essay addresses a unique topic, but all are anchored by keen observations of the environment and musings on alternative solutions to pressing environmental problems."

—FOREWORD REVIEWS

"Part memoir, part conservation treatise, and part history lesson . . . Lawton's focus is on how human lives are urgently shaped by their connection to water, whether it is in pieces on her love for her favorite river, the Stanislaus in California; a past Native American community's connection to that same river; or the 1970s-era engineers who built the dam that inundated it and erased those connections."

—PUBLISHERS WEEKLY

"A collection of strong, smart, wise, and deeply knowledgeable essays on water in the West, what it means and has meant to the author throughout her life, and what it means to all of us who depend on nature—the biggest oasis of all—for our lives. I came away from this book better informed, deeply touched, and quietly recommitted to the work of living more gently in our fragile world."

—JULIA WHITTY, author of *Deep Blue Home*
and *The Fragile Edge*

"The essays in *The Oasis This Time* flow like tributaries in a desert river. They meander and eddy and braid. They offer respite and challenge. Rebecca Lawton, as both intimate friend and knowledgeable guide, takes the reader on a dynamic journey from Las Vegas to Alaska, from the Grand Canyon to Ottawa. Her musings on this beloved arid land and its water shimmer with wonder at the life around us—birds, birds, and more birds!—and within us, and burn with urgency."

—ANA MARIA SPAGNA, author of *Uplake*
and *The Luckiest Scar on Earth*

"I opened *The Oasis This Time* assuming I was going to read about water. But what I read about instead is thirst. In straightforward, sometimes rascally, prose, Lawton digs into all the ways we want to be satiated. Our thirst for adventure, for love, for power and control, for ambitious development with an often warped sense of 'progress.' Hers is a wake-up call, shaped by Lawton's deep knowledge and love of place, and mostly her commitment to waterways, streams and creeks and rivers and oceans. We need this book."

—DEBRA GWARTNEY, author of *Live Through This*
and *I'm a Stranger Here Myself*

"In a parched and burning land, humanity's crimes against fresh water stand out with increasing starkness as crimes against ourselves. Through deft, spirited storytelling, Rebecca Lawton faces with compassionate courage the painful truths of our defiled and dwindling waterways; *The Oasis This Time* bids us to nurture the vital wellsprings we have too long taken for granted."

—SARAH JUNIPER RABKIN, author and illustrator of
What I Learned at Bug Camp

"Rebecca Lawton brings a poet's eye to the landscapes she loves, but she is, at heart, a warrior. With every sentence she fiercely defends what remains, totals her losses, and moves on to the next critical confrontation. In the end *The Oasis This Time* offers us a surprising amount of hope. Hope that we can survive even the worst of mankind's depredations. Hope that this planet is more resilient than we ever imagined."

—ANDY WEINBERGER, author of
The Ugly Man Sits in the Garden

THE OASIS THIS TIME

LIVING AND DYING
WITH WATER IN THE WEST

Rebecca Lawton

TORREY HOUSE PRESS

SALT LAKE CITY • TORREY

Excerpt from "Requiem for Sonora," from *Selected Poems, 1969–1981*, by Richard Shelton, copyright 1982. Reprinted by permission of the University of Pittsburgh Press.

Epigraph from *The History of Clowns for Beginners*, copyright 1995 Joe Lee. Reprinted with permission of the author.

Excerpt from *On the Loose*, copyright 1967 Renny Russell. Reprinted with permission of the author.

Excerpts from Wesley Smith's oral history interview in Volume 9 Number 3 (Summer 1996) of the *Boatman's Quarterly Review*. Reprinted with permission of Grand Canyon River Guides, Inc.

Excerpt from *Cadillac Desert*, copyright 1986 Marc Reisner. Reprinted with permission of Penguin Random House LLC.

First Torrey House Press Edition, March 2019
Copyright © 2019 by Rebecca Lawton

Published by Torrey House Press
Salt Lake City, Utah
www.torreyhouse.org

International Standard Book Number: 978-1-937226-93-0
E-book ISBN: 978-1-937226-94-7
Library of Congress Control Number: 2018956435

Cover design by Kathleen Metcalf
Interior design by Rachel Davis
Distributed to the trade by Consortium Book Sales and Distribution

These essays include excerpts from articles published in the following journals.

"The Sentinels" from "In the Oasis," in *Tiny Lights: A Journal of Personal Essay*, Tiny Lights Publications, 2005, edited by Susan Bono.

"Send in the Clowns" from "Midnight at the Oasis," *Aeon*, https://aeon.co/, November 6, 2015, edited by Pamela Weintraub.

"A Lot to Learn" from "The Big Dam Era Is Not Over," *Undark*, https://undark.org/, July 27, 2016, edited by Jane Roberts.

"May All Beings Be Stoked" from "How to Develop a Spiritual Connection to Water," *The Wisdom Daily*, http://thewisdomdaily.com, April 3, 2017, edited by Elad Nehorai.

"The Lone Kayaker" from "Breaking the Rules Outdoors," *Aeon*, https://aeon.co/, July 25, 2016, edited by Pamela Weintraub.

"First Responders" from "Fire Victims Humbled, Awed by Generosity," *Press Democrat*, January 25, 2018, edited by Linda Castrone; and from *Pepperwood Field Notes*, https://www.pepperwoodpreserve.org/, November and December 2017, edited by Tom Greco.

"Where the Birds Are" from "Giving In," *Hunger Mountain: The VCFA Journal for the Arts*, http://hungermtn.org/, March 23, 2017, edited by Jennifer Gibbons.

"Widowmakers" from "Helping Wildlife Survive in the Heat," *Santa Rosa Press Democrat*, July 26, 2017, edited by Corinne Asturias.

"Three Days to Be Here" from "The Healing Power of Nature," *Aeon*, http://aeon.co/, September 6, 2017, edited by Pamela Weintraub.

"Fountain of Fountains" from "Birding the Burn," *Audubon*, http://www.audubon.org/, January 9, 2018, edited by Hannah Waters.

"The Oasis This Time" from "Midnight at the Oasis," *Aeon*, http://aeon.co/, November 6, 2015, edited by Pamela Weintraub; and from "How to Develop a Spiritual Connection to Water," *The Wisdom Daily*, http://thewisdomdaily.com/, April 3, 2017, edited by Elad Nehorai.

For my father, Russell E. Lawton,
who beamed us to the oasis

CONTENTS

Introduction   3

1. The Sentinels   7
2. Send in the Clowns   20
3. Seventeen Palms   37
4. A Lot to Learn   50
5. Inappropriation   64
6. May All Beings Be Stoked   76
7. The Lone Kayaker   90
8. First Responders   99
9. Where the Birds Are   117
10. Why We Call It Mourning   130
11. Widowmakers   142
12. Three Days to Be Here   152
13. Everybody Was So Nice   162
14. Fountain of Fountains   182
15. The Oasis This Time   194

Acknowledgments   199

I have watched the workings of Fortune; I know her genius for envious dealings with [Hu]Mankind; and I also know that her empire is most absolute over just those oases in life in which the victim fancies his sojourn the most delectable and most secure.

—Polybius, *Histories*, 146 BC

Let's keep each other alive. Let's help each other out here.

—Wesley Smith, Grand Canyon river guide, 1996

INTRODUCTION

WHAT CAN WE SAY ABOUT OASES? THAT THEY ARE LUSH and lifesaving refuges in landscapes that are otherwise harsh and apt to kill us. That they are rare. That we're crazy for them, to the point of spending billions to build them in places where they wouldn't last a day without our adding vast amounts of water. That we're willing to murder for them, commit environmental crimes to emulate them, and fly the world to worship at their feet. That we'll pour our hearts and souls into basking in their shade and sustenance with the little free time our schedules allow. It's no wonder. The oasis is a rarity among ecosystems, a unique gem in an inhospitable world—in the words of the inestimable *Oxford English Dictionary*, "a fertile spot in a desert where water is found." *Oasis* conjures up the true palm sanctuary, the frond-fringed, shady haven of our collective imagination. We've expanded that waking dream to embrace any river, spring, pocket of rainwater in bedrock, and natural pool resilient enough to survive in an otherwise waterless environment. In those shimmering rarities, we know that we find life.

A desert, not a vague concept, is technically an area receiving less than ten inches of rainfall a year. The word comes from the Latin *desertum*, "something left waste." In a geographer's lexicon, the world's largest somethings-left-waste reside at the poles, together totaling approximately ten million square miles of ice, snow, and tundra (in the Arctic) and bedrock (in the Antarctic). Next largest is the Sahara, nearly three-and-one-half million square miles of gravel plain, sand, and dune spread over thirteen countries and a quarter of the African continent. After that, the Arabian Desert: one million square miles reaching into six steadfastly arid countries. Equal to one-fifth the area of all the continents, often inhospitable due to extreme temperatures and lack of surface water, deserts lure us with their starkness. They also hold the unequaled possibility of stumbling onto natural oases. Some of the most alluring land- and water-forms on the planet have a brilliant cachet due to, not in spite of, their hostile surroundings.

Deserts have their sworn allies. "But oh my desert / yours is the only death I cannot bear," Richard Shelton writes in "Requiem for Sonora." (Edward Abbey chose Shelton's words for one of three epigraphs to his 1975 novel, *The Monkey Wrench Gang.* The other two were by Walt Whitman and Henry David Thoreau.) In the same poem, Shelton pens:

> and you lie before me
> under moonlight as if under water
> oh my desert
> the coolness of your face

Cool, yes—seasonally or by night. Lying *underwater,* though, not so much; no surprise that Shelton spins it into metaphoric moonlight-water. When the rare surface water does come, created in spring runoff from mountains or the outpouring of a thunderstorm or the brief season of monsoons, then, in those pockets, we do find the coolness of the desert's face. There, and in the oasis, where there may be a central pool of open water, the *hydric zone* that quenches the thirst of desert travelers. Surrounding it stands the *true oasis*, or ring of water-dependent shrubs and trees—often palms. That circle or band of wet-zone plants lies within the outlying desert plants of the *ecotone*. Unique and eccentric shrubs of the ecotone are armed with spikes and claws, buffering the oasis proper like mean streets surrounding a glittering downtown. Even taken together, those three precious zones hold a tiny share in the vast expanse of our deserts. The oasis exerts its global influence in a matter of a few square miles rather than millions.

The bulk of these essays I wrote in my longtime home in Sonoma Valley, at my desk in the house I built with my husband, Paul Christopulos, on a wooded piece of streamside property he'd owned for decades. We found peace there, a neighborhood, friends, work, community, love. In the months in which I was finishing *The Oasis This Time*, we were preparing to leave for my new job in central Oregon. It would be a return to my birth state and a departure from a beloved place where we'd put down deep roots. Paul and I both raised our children in Sonoma, separately. We met through our shared passion for music and writing. Still I felt drawn back toward the wild places that had shaped my youth. Paul was open to a new journey, too. Now we're living on a slim, fragile margin between the Cascade Mountains and the Great Basin, a place we barely know and hardly expected to find. There's a familiar feeling to the not knowing—a memory of first trips on rivers and in canyons that later felt like home.

Thoreau wrote, "In wildness is the preservation of the world." No truer words have been written, or at least none that ring more true to our city- and town-weary ears. Now, on a planet that's undergoing increased desertification due to extended drought and heat, with water the limiting factor to wild and domestic populations, I see this sentiment and raise it. In the wildness of the natural oasis, in the sanctity of well-watered refuge, is the preservation of our beautiful, beleaguered world.

Rebecca Lawton
Summer Lake, Oregon

1.

THE SENTINELS

THE TOWN OF TWENTYNINE PALMS, CALIFORNIA, IS AS hushed as a morgue. Chairs sit empty in barbershops advertising marine haircuts for ten bucks. There are no families in the shops and cafés, no moms holding kids by the hand— just a quiet, Mojave Desert main street with traffic passing through. In a wind that hasn't given up its spring chill, yellow ribbons stream from light poles, street signs, storefronts. They're a faithful promise to endure, based on a pop song once played to death on the radio. The faded ribbons, bleached white on folds and curls, say that the waiting has gone on too long. Among stubby stands of sage and creosote, houses stand with drapes drawn to the ever-present sun. Inside, the residents must still be holding vigil, believing in the inevitable return of the warrior.

Lured by the call of anything wet, I check into the first motel I see. I find my air-conditioned room, pull on my bathing suit, wrap up in a big white towel, and wander out the back door in search of a hot tub.

A young marine greets me from a bistro table beside the water. He's a junior officer, probably just a few years older than my own teenaged daughter. His face reveals no guile, especially when he smiles. He tells me he's been assigned to an advanced course in communications.

He also volunteers an answer to the unasked question. "The base is dead quiet because everyone's overseas." He's stuck in town while others in his unit have been sent to Iraq.

Although the water is lovely and inviting, he has his back to it—he's in uniform, with a textbook spread before him. When he's done with his course, he'll ship out, too. The reading doesn't bother him, except that it requires "too much math." He says it in all earnestness, with no irony about the key role of numbers in his job. To him, they pose just one more barrier to getting to fight.

When I tell him I'm visiting from the northern part of the state, he asks if I've heard about a tank crew lost near Nasiriyah, Iraq. After some back and forth, I realize that I have: the gunner, a Scottish-born newlywed, lives close to my longtime home-town near San Francisco. The local paper has run a series on his going missing. His wife is expecting their first child any day.

"It's an M1A1 Abrams crew," he tells me. "They're based here, in Twentynine Palms."

I ask if he has updates. He does. The remaining members of the First Tank Battalion have no clue to the missing crew's whereabouts. The last radio contact from the Abrams came in before midnight Tuesday, when the tank was patrolling with-out headlights west of the Euphrates River. Today is Thursday. Desert sandstorms and near-zero visibility have made search efforts impossible. Blowing sand has confined the rest of the battalion to their quarters. Photographs in the paper show the men praying together in a dimly lit building.

"Doesn't it scare you?" I ask. "That an entire tank and its crew can disappear like that?"

The officer shakes his head. "Going MIA is one risk you take. And casualties are part of combat."

My heart beats so hard I wonder if he can hear it. Probably not. He goes back to his books with the calm of a Zen priest.

Should I pray? Make a wish? Some months ago a friend

taught me a time-tested method for wishing: fix your gaze on the nearest natural object and compose an eight-syllable blessing. My eyes go to a row of palm trees in the motel garden. I count out syllables on both hands. *Please. Find the crew. Alive and well.*

I unwrap from my towel and settle into the hot tub. Occasionally I check on the officer out of the corner of my eye. Now he's pressing buttons on his calculator, writing on a notepad, flipping through the textbook. He's eager, clearly, but how can he be so calm? As a Colorado River guide in the 1970s, I spent years working among veterans just home from fighting in Southeast Asia: former US Navy Seals, US Army Special Forces, US Marine Corps Enlisted—they could no more consider shipping out again than they could walk on water.

The hot-tub jets time out. The officer lifts his head. "Don't get up. I'll take care of it." He speaks with dignity, as if bearing a torch of responsibility for his mother or a favorite aunt.

I let him handle it for me.

I'VE COME TO THE DESERT FOR THE WATERS: SPECIFICALLY oases. My heart has been captured by spring-fed groves of California fan palm since I was in grade school. Whispering *Washingtonia filifera*, hiding in canyons. Their secretive ways. During most spring breaks, although we lived two states away, our parents drove south from our home outside Portland, Oregon, through the days and into the nights, with four little kids in the backseat. South from the Columbia River, down the Willamette Valley, with snow-draped Cascade Mountains to the east. South through the Central Valley with the Sierra Nevada rising up from greening foothills. We skirted Los Angeles as best we could. Mostly we kids read comic books while our parents did all the work, found some campsite or motel with space every night, and made sure we were fed, clean, and not bickering. Destination: Palm Canyon Campground,

Anza-Borrego Desert State Park east of San Diego, an arid haven of picnic tables under palm-frond *palapas* and windbreaks constructed of rock dug from nearby alluvial fans.

Most days we hiked up Palm Canyon or some other trail into the desert hills. The paths wound past white-blossomed agave, red fans of blooms on the ocotillos, waxy petals of flowers on the prickly pear cactus. We paused in awe when we caught a glimpse of a coyote's tail as it fled or picked out herds of desert bighorn sheep from cliffs they matched exactly. We endured the bird obsession of our mother, the times she stopped without warning to scan an inauspicious shrub with binoculars. She did manage eventually to make passionate birders of her husband and a few of her children; at the time, though, we small ones had little patience for standing statue-still to glimpse a nesting oriole or cactus wren.

Back then in Palm Canyon, most of the trees had long, full frond skirts, untouched by fire. Subsequently the trees were set ablaze by "careless" hikers, according to today's state park signs. Back then, though, the rustle of palm fronds set the soundscape. No traffic noise. Few human voices. A clear-running stream fell over boulders, pooled in little basins, ran free over pebbles and gravel. Here there were no school tests, no student cliques, no yearning for recess. Who even had thoughts of going home? The oasis became a cherished refuge, a place where every molecule of water in our bodies could rest among peaceful canopies of *Washingtonia*.

AT THE ENTRANCE TO JOSHUA TREE NATIONAL PARK, 130 miles northeast of our beloved Anza-Borrego and one mile from downtown Twentynine Palms, stands a tiny palm oasis of the same numerical name. A fertility legend attached to it endures, repeated in newspapers, motel advertisements, and desert-rat tour books. It's a mythical place not to be missed, the accounts say. The oasis is the town's forebear, a stopover for travelers since prehistoric times. On my second morning in the area, I cross the motel lobby on my way out to find the storied refuge. Through gleaming windows, I spot the officer at work again by the pool and think immediately of the missing tank crew. Headlines in the motel's newspaper rack tell me nothing. Hoping for good news later, I duck out to conduct my search: a short drive, a nearly empty parking lot at the National Park Service visitor center, a paved path to well-tended stands of *Washingtonia*.

In movies filmed in the desert, desperate, thirst-crazed pilgrims plunge into oases headfirst. The ubiquitous presence of water belies the fact that an oasis may not be wet at all. The hydric zone may be a spring or pool, true, but it is just as likely to be wet earth indicating groundwater near the surface. Here there is neither pool nor dampness. There's no open pool anywhere, no yearned-for expanse of blue. Not only that, the surrounding oasis proper isn't the obvious circle of palms, the stuff of kneeling camels and silk-swathed sheikhs. Instead, just a few palms string along the trails here—hardly a circle, at least not at first glance. The third and outer zone, the desert-oasis ecotone, is sparse. It's not so different from the surrounding desert that lurks like a cruel bar bouncer on the outside of the precious palms.

Later I'll read that the marshy, ecologically diverse center of the Twentynine Palms oasis dried up some thirty years ago. Declines in groundwater desiccated the springs watering vegetation and wildlife. Monitoring of groundwater wells by the California Department of Water Resources has shown the impact of a training base, a town, and the visitation of over 140,000 souls annually. Between 1939 and 2013, water levels dropped seventy feet and more beneath Twentynine Palms.

Even without open water, the little shade of the oasis beckons. Visitors are fenced out, though, because the weight of our trespass would damage the trees' root systems. *Washingtonia* has pencillate rootlets just inches underground that reach as far as twenty feet from the trunk. Their job is to search for shallow groundwater. Too many pedestrians, no matter how appreciative our hearts, would trample and compress the soil supporting the vulnerable network. The palms are therefore barred with handrails and threats of hefty fines. We spectators stick to the trails and hold onto our cash.

Even with the park's best efforts, the trees at Twentynine Palms fail to send their shallow roots to moisture. The water table has simply dropped too far. To keep the oasis alive, National Park Service staff regularly apply water directly to the base of the palms. They irrigate.

Interpretive signs further the fertility legend, as well as a second name for the oasis: *Mara* or *Marah*, meaning "big springs and much grass." The word derives from Native American lexis—probably the Serrano language. In the legend, indigenous women of the Mojave traveled to the oasis specifically to give birth to sons. Archaeological studies may not support that, but they do document habitation by Native Americans in the area, first Serrano and Cahuilla then Chemehuevi, millennia before it became a base for men about to wage war. Footpaths radiate out from the once abundantly marshy Mara, a hub of prehistoric comings and goings. A count of 480 bone fragments in excavations at the site evidence a prehistoric human diet of largely black-tailed jackrabbit and desert tortoise, as well as lesser amounts of desert bighorn sheep, mule deer, smaller mammals, birds, and reptiles. For a time, a settlement near Mara served as home or camp for those foraging the nearby alluvial fans and hills.

The total number of palms at Mara, however, has not been recorded as twenty-nine; rather, oral and written accounts beginning in the 1800s note fewer than twenty. Even at the time of European contact, palms numbered in the teens.

Still, the legend says that sometime around 1500 AD,

spiritual advisors or "medicine men" directed women who wanted male children to Mara. Blessed by shade in a land that had little, the palmgrove Mecca also had sweet water with reputed supernatural properties. Mara, the family clinic of the ancient world. The hopeful migrations to the oasis must have succeeded. In the first year alone, the legend says, expectant mothers who visited the oasis were delivered of twenty-nine male babies. They reportedly celebrated by planting one palm at the site for each infant boy. The trees they sowed grew tall, becoming guideposts visible over great distances. Only later did this same haven take on another type of maleness: a training ground for soldiers headed for oil-fueled battle in foreign deserts.

Thinned by fire in some places and trampled in others, the *Washingtonia* at Mara still summon visitors, murmuring veiled invitations.

We want sons, they might be saying. *Bring us sons.*

I walk the park service paths thinking of the pregnant women who may have blazed trails here. Strolling paths now paved and widened, I stop at a handrail to gaze into the hydric zone. This is the famous Oasis of Mara. This patch of sand and struggling palms. The formerly biodiverse, reputedly damp refuge is largely mesquite and *Washingtonia*.

Years later, on March 26, 2018, Mara was dealt another blow, when local resident and paroled arsonist George William Graham set fire to the palms. He played God with the remaining trees, taking a black BIC lighter to these besieged two and a half acres. Several stressed, historic palms were destroyed along with a few other remnant plant species. Reminders of a greater spectrum of wildlife and once-vibrant lineage of ancient people went up in swirls of ash. Park rangers arrested Graham as he stuck around to watch the blaze.

⁓

ON DAY THREE I RISE BEFORE DAWN TO EXPLORE ANOTHER oasis named for a tally of palms. Outside town, *Washingtonia* still grows naturally at springs and along fault lines in narrow canyons. That's the case at Fortynine Palms, a 1.5-mile walk from a trailhead not far from my motel. I make the short drive; I reach the lot at daybreak. The day's new sun throws beams over the facing ridge. Granite boulders shine beside the trail. Flakes of mica flash in the sand before my boots. Ridges along flanks of mountains shed light so that alluvial fans throw shadows. It's a brilliant morning.

Fortynine Palms strings before me, a green necklace. The oasis has a narrow hydric zone in a long, arid arroyo. Fresh water tickles among horsetails, maidenhair fern, willow, and cottonwood where a small bit of flow is enough to fill tiny, clear pools. Glassy surfaces are topped by gaggles of water striders. A buzz fills the air as life stirs with the sun. Hummingbirds dive-bomb in mating dances and zoom into blossoms on scattered stands of globe mallow. Gnatcatchers and orioles call, and the sweet scent of things growing permeates the morning.

With every step closer to the water source, I find more surprises. A stippled cluster of doglike prints of coyotes at mud-rimmed pools, signs of a pack that's come and gone. Scat stuffed with bones and palm seeds. The California fan palm is not a date tree, but its small, black fruit still lures many creatures, including large mammals. Watch out, California and Gambel's quail—you could end up in the jaws of a hunting *Canis latrans*.

Moisture from below the surface seeps into my bootprints. It's a life-giving aspect of these narrow canyons, their wet backbones. Here, groundwater lurks beneath the barest skin of gravel and sand. Alternately, in the rainy months, too much water may rip through here—high, fast, and sudden. A storm far up the drainage may drench bedrock, then send snouts of muddy runoff through narrow, shotgun canyons. Flash floods roar and rip and uproot. They're the leading killer of California fan palms in tight, rock-bound arroyos. Not death by drying, as one might think, or the trampling of young palm pups under heavy hiking boots.

Rather, it's the screaming, wild, rain-fed flood that upends elder palms and carries off seedlings, prying loose their shallow roots. Only the most sheltered and strongest survive these torrents that rise out of nowhere, churn through, and only spare trees if they're protected by a random boulder or arm of alluvial fan. The mud floods leave silty scars on remaining trees, dozens of feet above ground. Look up in a palm canyon and you're bound to see high-water marks far overhead.

Death by water in the desert: one of nature's greatest ironies.

As the day's heat mounts at Fortynine Palms, the music of birds fades. Insect drone takes over as bees of all sizes work the willow catkins. Two pair of quail pick at creosote and bob their way up-canyon, their loose-necked march mostly hidden beneath dry-channel canopy. I creep onto a boulder to let them pass. Three quail rely for safety on a fourth bird who perches on a pile of stones to serve as sentry. I hold my breath. The birds' jerky, searching movements take them past, apparently without seeing me, until they all turn without warning toward my right foot. Everything goes fine for a moment, until one bird reaches my boot, the sentry cries, and all four scatter like tossed dice.

The boot that scared them off looks harmless to me. Past it, however, I find something in the pink granite gravel that's shiny and not always so harmless—a single rifle shell, resting near my toes on the gravel-bottomed wash. Luckily the shell is a casing, spent and empty. As I study it, a jet fighter stealth-flies like a harrier overhead, throwing shadow. The aircraft rips away with a roar.

WASHINGTONIA, IMPERATIVE TO LIFE IN THE MOJAVE, HAS AS its doppelgänger the genus *Phoenix* in the Persian Gulf. Like the California fan palm, the highly cultivated, date-bearing *Phoenix* needs full sun, heat, and scads of subsurface water. *Phoenix* has long brought wealth and status to its growers, because there's no end to what you can do with the tree. You can cut its fronds for shelter. You can weave its mature leaves into mats, screens, baskets, and crates. You can strip off its fruit clusters to prepare the fronds for brooms or weave palm fiber into skirts and sandals. The high-tannin date fruit has cured everything from intestinal troubles to alcoholic intoxication through the ages.

Even if palm fruit doesn't cure hangover, as implied, the *Phoenix* tree of the Middle Eastern oasis stands for food, fiber, firewood. Survival for desert dwellers.

Ancient Mesopotamians encouraged *Phoenix* to grow at scattered hydric zones by planting them there and protecting the growth of young palm pups. Communities depended on the trees they had fostered. Honored in myth and mirage and a thousand Arabian nights, the date palm stood from time unknown in the wedge of land between the Tigris and Euphrates Rivers. Archaeological evidence of cultivars goes back to four thousand years before Christ. In a way, *Phoenix* is a messiah in its own right—abundant in its gifts, revered in the earliest bas-relief sculpture, exalted on the faces of antiquated coins.

A wonder tree. Own a palm, own the world.

Because the trees are critical to life both in and out of the oasis, they are strategic targets in times of war. *Phoenix* lore holds that in the 1824 siege of Suckna, a station on the caravan route between Mesopotamia and central Syria, the conqueror Abdel-Gelil cut down more than forty thousand trees to compel the town to surrender. The campaign worked, and the scorched-palm tactic has been used in many conflicts since to gain dominance over populations. For the Iraqi people, who have long led the world in date production, the much-harassed *Phoenix* has become a military Achilles' heel. Iraqis, wise and hardworking stewards of *Phoenix*, develop many of the most popular cultivars, including those bearing soft, sweet Halawy and Khadrawy fruits. Then, standing tall, holding the bread of life and unable to hide in an exposed landscape, the generous palm falls in mute capitulation when the enemy comes swinging sabers.

We in the West have done more than our share to destroy the palm in the Tigris-Euphrates. Iraq's forty million commercial trees had already come under attack in the 1980s' Iran-Iraq War. Sometime during the descent of allied forces in the 1991 Gulf War, numbers of palms registered just fifteen million. After September 11, 2001, Allied forces again invaded Iraq, albeit years later: US and British air strikes that began on March 20, 2003, and continued for three weeks coincided with and interrupted palm fertilization to Iraq's remaining ten million trees. Little has been written in Western news about the destruction of palms north of Baghdad in 2003, but newspapers from the area reported invading armies bulldozing farmers' trees to extract information about guerrilla insurgents. In 2005, Iraq's annual output of dates, usually twenty to thirty tons, was slim enough to only meet children's needs and provide dessert for growers' guests. In 2006, the same newspapers reported that any surviving trees were expected to be barren.

Exterminate the date palm, and you take a knife to the throats of its people. Kill the tree that rims the oasis, and you help bring Algerians, Moroccans, Tunisians, Egyptians, Arabians, Iranians, and Iraqis to their knees.

WAR FOUND MARA, TOO, COMING IN ON THE ANCIENT NATIVE footpaths. After the shelter and open water drew miners, homesteaders, cattlemen, and the stage line, small outposts gradually coalesced into the village of Twentynine Palms. No longer the sacred destination for mothers desiring to make sons, it drew the sons themselves. Most men arriving there had either just returned from war or were about to go. Veterans of World War

I who'd suffered lung problems during the gassing in France came to the clean, dry air to regain the power to breathe. Mara became life itself, with long horizons and unbroken sunlight. Basins of rock and sand, a world away from the mud and gloom of trench warfare and the dark, northern forests of Europe, meant a return from the dark side of the moon.

When World War II loomed, the US military found the open skies of Twentynine Palms ideal for glider instruction. The Navy expanded that use into an auxiliary air station that later transferred to the Marine Corps. The Semper Fi have live-fire trained there with no breaks since 1953. No rest for the warrior in either war or peace.

RETURNING TO TOWN, I'M JONESING FOR MORE HOT-TUB TIME and maybe even an umbrella drink beside the swimming pool. Aglow from hiking, I pass through the motel lobby and catch sight of a headline on a newspaper in the media rack. Buying a paper, I detour to a plush chair in the lobby. TANK CREW FOUND. The oversized font usually reserved for presidential election upsets and fires that force evacuations now applies to the team of men who trained right here only months ago.

When the Abrams was finally located, it was by Navy divers in twenty feet of Euphrates River water. Somehow disoriented even after the sandstorm cleared, the driver missed a turn and plunged off the end of an unfinished bridge. The tank flipped, its turret and escape hatch shoving into soft river mud. Trapped inside the Abrams, all four crew members perished.

The Scotsman's pregnant wife is brave as she faces the reporters from regional and national newspapers. "He loved his job," she says of her deceased husband. "It totally fit him." She's showing huge composure and keeping things brief. There are no hints about risk. Nothing about the irony of death in a desert river. Reading her words, I want nothing more than to find the communications officer. I rush to the swimming pool to discover he's still at his post. He looks up from his math with a quick smile. His face fills with the light of recognition.

I ask if he's heard about the tank crew. He has. The news has only firmed his resolve to join his unit. His expression turns solemn. "I want to go soon. I don't want to be like a prizefighter who trains day in and day out for two years and never gets to go in the ring."

The thought of him taking the blows suffered by pugilists, both in and out of the ring, hurts my heart. I try not to let my face show it as we fall into a tentative silence. It's a fool's desire to think that he might keep his wide-eyed, shining look. His young brain is still maturing, still growing its ability to reason. Only when he's lived to the ripe old age of twenty-six, I've read, will his nervous system be considered adult. Only then will he recognize life's warning lights, like the oil lamps on car dashboards that stop us from driving into danger. Risky behavior is especially attractive to a certain demographic, specifically Caucasian males under the age of twenty-five with high school educations or less. This young officer may qualify on all counts, but I won't ask. Neither is he about to bring it up.

He goes back to his math. I don't fold him in a protective embrace, but someone should. Should I pray? Or make a second wish? With my gaze on the motel palms again, I compose another eight-syllable blessing: *Please. Survive fire and water.*

He keeps his vigil with the books. The face of the pool shimmers. It's groundwater, Mara-sustaining liquid, pumped out of soil and rock and into the desert air. Taking my place in the hot tub, within the hydric zone in this otherwise arid garden, I hold a vigil of my own.

2.

Send in the Clowns

Chaos and order, yin and yang, Abbott and Costello.

—Joe Lee, author, cartoonist, and student
of the former Ringling Brothers and Barnum
& Bailey Clown College in Sarasota, Florida

MY FIRST VISIT TO LAS VEGAS: AN OVERNIGHT WITH MY mother, father, and siblings on a road trip home from Arizona. We'd hauled across three states in our old Chevy station wagon, my father driving, my mother navigating. We four kids crowded into the backseat, maybe one of us in the seatless *way back*. It had been a wandering break from our home in rainy Oregon, the kind of trip we all loved. We'd milked the best out of every campground we'd found in the Mojave and Sonoran Deserts, often dry camping where no one else had pulled off. The nights sparkled with stars. The songs of coyote packs edged the dark. While our folks slept on a plywood bed in the wagon, we kids lay out under a shelter of sky, with only the thin layers of well-worn cotton sleeping bags between us and the godforsaken wilderness. They were more than enough.

When we entered Las Vegas's orbit, we were still in thrall of the natural wonders of the Grand Canyon. We'd gotten dusty in mining and farming towns. We'd hung out on wooden porches in Old Tucson, were *right there* when outlaws challenged each other in the dirt streets. By contrast, the city had the shimmer of mirage. A fantasy of flickering lights—at first beckoning, but then proving hard and gray and dirty with littered streets.

We stayed less than twenty-four hours, arriving at dusk one day and leaving after breakfast the next. I remember just one, vivid episode during that small window of time. Our family of six was returning to our motel room via a concrete alleyway. My folks were out in front of us kids. Maybe we had our shoulders hunched to the chaos. Maybe we'd just left a 1960s version of today's All-You-Can-Eat casino dinner. For sure we got a good look at the unglamorous posteriors of businesses backed onto the alley. Only a few other tourists walked there, hurrying past, dressed up for the foreign landscape in suits and heels. Slot machines jingled and whirled wherever a casino door stood open. The sounds matched the strangeness of the sights.

Down the alley, far toward the end, a man worked the sidewalk with a wide broom. Even from a distance, I could tell he wore some kind of costume. From billboards, I'd gathered that Las Vegas traded in disguise—women in jewels and feathers, adults with mask-like faces wearing perpetually excited looks as they watched outpourings of coins from slot machines. I stayed behind my parents and close to my older siblings—for once my place as third child didn't bother me. We strolled nearer the sweeper. As we came into range, I stole the inevitable look. He was a sad-faced clown. He wore a suit of rags, battered derby, oversized tie, and big, floppy shoes.

He kept complete focus on his work. His alley-sweeping was not a performance. If not that, then what was it? He was really cleaning up. Maybe even the janitors were part of the act in this strange, out-of-place place in the middle of the Nevada desert.

WHAT HAPPENS HERE, STAYS HERE. IT'S THE LAS VEGAS CREED, a promise of anonymity for the visitor. The slogan is world renowned, the place considered a port in any storm. In the

1990s, the city had billed itself as a family-friendly destination, but that tack just didn't cut it. Kids weren't proving to be the big-ticket customers that their adult gambling counterparts could be. A casino host puts it this way: "I have a guy go to the pool and dump like seventy-eight thousand dollars in three minutes. He didn't win a hand. It was brutal, right?" Meanwhile dads and moms, out of necessity, might dodge any come-ons as they shepherd the kids to the discounted buffet.

"Las Vegas needed a new direction," the advertising agency R&R wrote in 2002 for the Las Vegas Convention and Visitors Authority, "for positioning the brand that would tap into the visceral and deeply emotional reasons visitors connect with the city."

How visceral? No less than the fundamentally American entitlement to independence. How emotional? Our very need for liberty. Drawing on "rigorous brand research and analytics," R&R concluded that people come to Las Vegas yearning to breathe free. "Adults get tired of adulting from time to time and desperately need some 'Adult Freedom'—in a place where they won't be judged." In Las Vegas, one's conduct needed to be off the record. The campaigners called the new spin a *code, insight, tagline, cause, message, cultural phrase, platform, voice, spark, strategy*—by any other name, it was branding. A business proposition.

It worked. R&R's campaign and tagline entered the fabric of American culture, went worldwide, and "produced some of the most celebrated work in all of advertising." The Visitors Authority saw a seventeen-to-one return on advertising dollars; year-round hotel occupancy rate boosted to eighty-seven percent, twenty-two percent above the national average; doubling of annual visitation from about twenty-one million guests in the kiddie era to forty-two million in 2016. Recognition in the media. "A stroke of marketing genius" (*The New York Times*). "A cultural phenomenon" (*Advertising Age*).

Uniforms for staff at most casinos morphed from those of dirndled, kid-friendly storybook characters to bikini tops and tight, revealing pirate's pantaloons. Money and water flowed on the four-plus-mile reach of boulevard known as The Strip with a newfound sense of abundance. Families still could find plenty to do, but mostly at Circus Circus, which continued to flash the face of Lucky the Clown on its neon marquee. Fodor's Travel dubbed the Circus Circus Adventuredome as "a welcome oasis in the frenzied Vegas adult scene." Otherwise, Las Vegas itself became known as a rest stop away from the demands of parenting, running a household, working nine-to-five, and otherwise grinding on the wheel of daily obligation.

A FRIEND I'LL CALL MIKE RECENTLY SHARED THE STORY OF the power of Las Vegas to lure grownups into its cool embrace. Mike's father, "Richard," had reached his nineties after serving in the public sector, retiring in a wealthy suburb of Los Angeles, and inheriting a fortune in California real estate from parents and siblings. Richard also had acquired three marriages over the years: the first to Mike's mother (ending in divorce), the second to a successful, working wife (lasting until her death), and the third to a much-younger, struggling single mother.

When I met Richard in his eighties, he walked with a limp and the uneven posture of a man suffering from scoliosis. He was quiet, mostly listening during conversation and responding with few words. He did have alive, interested eyes. When Mike saw him at his ninetieth birthday party in Los Angeles, though, Richard had become homebound. There was no more talk of the world travel he'd done with his third wife, "Annie." Instead, the age gap between them had grown too wide to cross.

"One night Annie called me," Mike says, "and was kind of hysterical, saying that Dad was in the hospital doing really, really badly, and was in Las Vegas. She said, 'I'm giving you a chance to see your father' before he dies." Mike felt the sting of her words but wasn't surprised. Annie had become Richard's gatekeeper in recent years. Gradually, with a little-girl voice and manner that Mike describes as timid, she'd encouraged Richard to bond with her daughters and their string of live-in boyfriends.

Still, Mike wanted to see his father. He arranged a flight the next day to Las Vegas. Annie called in the morning to say he was too late. Richard had passed in the night.

"Yeah, thanks," Mike recalls thinking, "but what were the circumstances of his death? What was he even doing in Vegas? Why would anyone load a ninety-something man that frail into a car to drive him all that way?"

Mike still doesn't know, but he suspects it had something to do with Annie's own addiction to Glitter Gulch. She'd often flown to Las Vegas to see a good friend there during her marriage to Richard. "Here's Annie, my age or younger, and Dad's an old man. I'd suspected some sort of romance, because she'd take off and go there alone. Maybe Dad even knew about it and was okay with it."

At Richard's wake, Mike met the "friend," a private contractor who worked for several casinos. "His job was to keep their best customers happy. He'd give gamblers little tchotchkes and a free meal here and there and make them feel like they're big shots. Basically he was paid to build people like Annie up. It began to dawn on me that she'd been going to Vegas to gamble, and was probably gambling away all of Dad's wealth. She led kind of a double life."

Mike finds it ironic that Richard had been in Vegas at all. "He was very anti-gambling. There was some story about his own father betting away what little money he had. Dad wasn't one of those people who 'goes to Vegas.' He thought it was stupid. He never wanted to go."

∼

I know something about adult freedom. The Grand Canyon river trips I worked in the 1970s and '80s took people out of their day-to-day and into a different world—a deep, barely accessible place both physically and in the realm of regular human experience. The few dozen or so passengers on every trip unwound as they never did on the other rivers I worked in four other states. The letting go wasn't something prescribed by river management. You couldn't read about it in the advertising. Several days into a trip, someone might say, "This wasn't mentioned in your company's brochure." The unbinding of souls came from an authentic immersion into a mile-deep place with astounding sights, monumental whitewater, rock walls so tall they inspired constant awe, and desert nights of unequaled tranquility. The physical factors combined, basically, to enchant everyone who made the trek. Bonding was inevitable, born of beauty as well as a feeling of hard-earned accomplishment in getting to camp safely at the end of every day. It took teamwork to make our way through that big, honking gorge, no matter how many times we'd run it.

River canyons, especially the Grand Canyon, are places of secrets, too: hidden green grottoes never dreamed of by the sun-dazed visitor who spends the obligatory ten minutes at the South Rim; unexpected friendships, cemented by the cooperation needed to get down 224 miles of world-class wild river.

Once back in the real world, we didn't talk much about how a trip had gone. There were the usual disclosures about screwed-up or aced runs through rapids, but other trip descriptions fell short. Not so much because we wanted to keep it quiet as to acknowledge that words could never do the place or the people justice. We could take a stab at describing the chiaroscuroed walls, the complete immersion into a natural wonder, the kick-ass waves produced by changing debris fans and inscrutable gneiss narrows, but we couldn't explain how we'd been changed. We just knew that the place cast a spell.

We'd been to a dwelling of solace and sanctuary, and we wanted to return again and again.

SOMETIMES ON THE GRAND CANYON TRIPS, A GUIDE OR PAS-senger had to hike out—to go back to a job somewhere, to end the season and return to school, to resupply something *very* important, like toilet paper or wound sutures or beer. In that case, usually still in summer's doggiest days, it was a grueling journey to the rim. A race with the sun. The hiker would start before daylight, carrying all the filtered river water he could manage. For his own sake, he'd have to get out before most tourists at the rim rose for breakfast. A hiker had to zoom up the Bright Angel Trail to the Devil's Corkscrew (a wall of switchbacks near the top) with as little dehydration drama as possible. He'd bolt the 6.3 miles up to Indian Garden, where clean water was available to fortify him for the remaining 1.2 miles to the rim. "Indian Garden is an oasis in the canyon used by Native Americans up to modern times," the National Park Service writes. The garden makes Bright Angel Trail the safest of all possible hiking routes from the canyon, due to "potable water, regular shade, and emergency phones."

Going from an oasis like Indian Garden to an oasis like South Rim isn't just a hiker's invention; water sources on des-ert treks have been key to human evolution since our very first years. The earliest people lived and hunted in arid lands, travel-ing between rare springs and pools where plant sources of food grew and wildlife foraged and stalked. Anthropological digs of *Homo sapiens* in Olduvai Gorge, Tanzania, included paleonto-logical evidence of isolated oases. Our forebears lived on the rare freshwater body, then traveled to the next one, especially during wet years, ultimately finding their way out of Africa.

Oases likewise determined the trajectory of trade routes and settlement sites. The 4,600-mile Silk Road through Africa, Asia, and Europe strung together water sources leading to and from communities like Turpan in China and Samarkand in Uzbekistan. There was the Darb el-Arba'in camel route in middle Egypt and the Sudan. The Moroccan caravan path from the Niger to Tangier. The aboriginal foot trails in the Mojave Desert in the American Southwest. Separate bodies of water, sometimes miniscule, connected us.

Later, the built world borrowed key ingredients of the oasis to bolster community life. The water creed in Rome, *In Aqua Sanitas*, promoted immersion for recuperation, rejuvenation, and improved citizenship. Be a good Roman. Clean up and calm down in the baths. Elaborate systems of aqueducts led from rivers and springs to towns and villages to fill the *balneae* (small-scale public and private baths) and *thermae* (large-scale, Imperial baths). In these community centers of their time, citizens gathered for conversation, soaks, and massage.

Water, central to restoring the human spirit, was already imported from the wilderness.

So water flows from the Grand Canyon to Las Vegas today. From one adult playground to another, from its Rocky Mountain headwaters to its impoundment at Glen Canyon and Hoover Dams, the Colorado River helps supply the immense human need to recuperate. In so harnessing the water flowing between stone walls, we see it not as a river. We've invented language for its incomparable need to *go* somewhere, and ours: *flow regimes, bypass tunnels, turbines, releases,* and *cubic feet per second.*

MY FAMILY PUT LAS VEGAS BEHIND US, BUT THE MYSTERY OF the alley-sweeping clown stayed with me. A puzzle. Clowns around the globe have evolved on a long and wandering trajectory from trickster to fool to star entertainers under the big top. *Trickster* comes from the French *triche,* from *trichier,* "to deceive." *Fool* derives from the Latin *foilis,* for "bellows" or "windbag" (and, some say, "scrotum"). Trickster is the one who slaps; the fool is the one slapped. The clown does both, giving as good as he gets, surprising us when he first trips and falls like a doofus but then jumps up to demonstrate he's the best bareback rider in three states.

The television clowns I'd known before that evening in Las Vegas showed little inhibition—they'd sob at the death of a flea. They'd shoot water from a flower. Their single handkerchief would grow to a laundry line. The inscrutable man in face paint might do anything at any moment. Decades after walking with my family down that alleyway, whenever I'd stop at the Hopi mesas between river trips, the dancing clowns in the pueblos would be there, in costume, under the hot sun. Families sat in surrounding seats, or stood on the walls looking down onto the dirt dance floor, watching. Sometimes quiet laughter would ripple through the audience, but whatever amused them flew over my head.

Now I think it was all about distraction. Obviously the clowns knew what they were doing—vying for the attention of serious dancers, making offers no one could refuse, playing to the crowd. While they sashayed seemingly without agenda among the other players, they were part of the act, and an important one. Throughout history, the key purpose of clowns has been to take our eyes off the ball. They spin straw into gold. They pull tricks out of a bottomless bag and then lift an umbrella and float out of sight. They exchange violent slaps and insults, then do that ridiculous thing of making sausage. We let ourselves be taken in. We're complicit.

While we're dazzled, they part us from our gold. We're feeling good, not so attached to our cash. We don't resist the gambler's sleight of hand even though our higher selves know it's there. In the words of Ecclesiastes 1:15, "The number of fools is infinite." Or, as P. T. Barnum famously did not say, "There's a sucker born every minute."

~

WATER THERAPY SPREAD FROM ROME TO OTHER PARTS OF the built world. In going global, it acquired an international lexicon. Spa, Belgium, is synonymous with the soak. So is the *bain* in France, *Toplice* in Slovenia, *Bad* in Germany, *fürdo* in Hungary, *città thermale* in Italy. Early adopters of the Roman tradition didn't have access to today's research, which shows that heart-deep immersion for just ten minutes in a tank of eighty-six-degree Fahrenheit water improves the ability of blood, full of oxygen and nutrients, to perfuse the brain. Immersion may be billed as luxury, but its positive effects on neurological function make it more essential health benefit than extravagance. Soaking helps us think straight.

The enhancement of shade at any oasis is key, too, natural or not. We (and other mammals) need a two- or threefold increase in natural evaporation to survive the desert sun. We bake out there, unless we have canopy to cool our sweat so we can keep going. Our minds, especially, need to chill out, as our brains stay about thirty-two degrees Fahrenheit hotter than the rest of us. That brain fog we feel under hot sun beating down through cloudless skies isn't imagined; it's real and measurable. If we were to listen to our hot heads—our overheated brains—we'd cease walking to the next oasis. We'd perish out there, become a parody, emulate the crawling, ragged victims in the magazine cartoons.

To bring us immersion and shade, today's spa towns install fountains and pools, plant trees brought in from exotic locales, and build dimly lit rooms to reimagine the shade of the natural oasis. The purpose: to help stimulate endorphins, morphine-like molecules associated with feelings of deep pleasure. Endorphins attach to "opiate" receptors in the body and brain. The forty-billion-dollar resort and spa industry, a fast-growing sector of leisure travel worldwide, knows about these feel-good results, and it's not shy in using water to get them. Hot tubs, steam rooms, mud baths, and other assorted water bodies are built for relaxation, rejuvenation, and recovery. The touch of water on bare skin at the end of a hard day? It feels like heaven, and heaven is the oasis.

The valley dubbed *Las Vegas* ("The Meadows") was known for its wealth of water long before the casinos offered Jacuzzi rooms alongside nickel slots with 93.42 percent odds (tops). "Oh! such water," settler Oliver Pratt wrote in 1848. "It comes . . . like an oasis in the desert just at the termination of a fifty-mile stretch without a drop of water or spear of grass." The Meadows has quenched human thirst for thirteen thousand years; it has sated wildlife for much longer. The natural artesian flow of the valley, though—once enough to "propel a grist mill with a dragger run of stones!" (exclamation mark courtesy of Pratt)—is a thing of the past.

The Meadows began desiccating in the 1800s with the advent of the railroad (steam engines needed a lot of H_2O) and the 1905 formation of the Las Vegas Land and Water Company. Growth followed, then military and industrial development, then gambling, then Boulder Dam and "Lake" Mead to water it all. A steady rise in population followed in the 1940s and '50s. About Las Vegas, the US Geological Survey writes in modern reports, "By 1962, the springs that had supported the Native Americans, and those who followed, were completely dry."

To recapture the precious, natural oasis ecosystem that had once characterized The Meadows, those supplying Las Vegas with water perform a sleight of hand that fits the illusory quality of the place. The Colorado River, harnessed at the dam that hoovers water toward Mead, fulfills eighty-six percent of the valley's water portfolio. Groundwater pumped from beneath the city and its sprawl supplies what the river cannot, contributing another ten percent to metropolitan and urban use. Recycled water makes up the last four percent. The Southern Nevada Water Authority estimates that casinos and resorts use an annual thirty-two thousand acre-feet of river water piped from Mead and four thousand acre-feet of groundwater from private wells (thirty-six thousand acre-feet in all, nearly twelve billion gallons).

With 603,000 residents within the city limits in the most recent census, and over two million in the greater metropolitan area—as well as *forty-two million annual visitors* brought in by successful advertising—the once-abundant surface and groundwater of the valley hasn't met Last Vegas's needs for years. Wells have been so systematically overdrawn that the water table has declined more than three hundred feet. The associated subsurface rock and soil, naturally hydrated when groundwater stays in the ground, has "deflated" and sunk some five feet in places. Resulting earthquakes, irreversible ground collapse, and property settling have caused billions of dollars worth of damage in the Las Vegas valley. Ground failures will worsen, says the US Geological Survey, as current use continues.

Far worse than any property damage is the sobering fact that, once depleted, groundwater won't replenish for millennia. In the Las Vegas valley, natural recharge of the aquifer system—or replenishment from rainfall permeating the subsurface soil and rock—ranges from twenty-five thousand to thirty-five thousand acre-feet annually (only a quarter to a third of the more than one hundred thousand acre-feet or thirty-three billion gallons of subsurface water that we withdraw each year). That the water balance sheet is out of whack is not a new trend. In 1911, Nevada State Engineer W. M. Kearney advised against the region's "lavish wasteful manner [with water], which has prevailed in the past." Not many took him seriously.

Where does all the water go? Largely toward the creation of faux oases. The Water Authority estimates that sixty percent of drinking-quality water delivered to homes and businesses in Las Vegas irrigates landscaping and fills water features. In short, more than half of water that could be left in the river or under ground spews into fountains and onto lawns. Some seventy percent of residential use and twenty percent of casino and spa use is applied outdoors, for landscaping and swimming pools, or evaporated with the gusto of any arid region. Water use in Las Vegas is largely *consumptive*—that is, it's fully used. It can't be treated and recycled to bolster that measly four percent of recycled water (which is great for landscaping) or reserved for the river ecosystem in return-flow credits (conserved acre-feet that go back on the river's side of the balance sheet). Consumptively used water is lost water.

So what? So Las Vegas is thirsty for more. The Water Authority is actively looking for new sources throughout Nevada. The US Geological Survey has said that piping water from the Virgin and Muddy Rivers to the north is a leading option for supplementing water-demand shortfalls in Vegas. Natural wetlands farther from The Meadows will be drained. Wetland species in remote reserves, like a species of tiny fish known as the Moapa dace, are already threatened by environmental changes that include drought. They hang on in little green refuges where one can stop to watch birds and wildlife, like the wetlands of the Desert National Wildlife Refuge Complex. If voracious Las Vegas has its way, such real oases may go dry.

And we play our part. We whose need for water is to this day lavish, we whose spirits soar at the sight of green in the desert, we who *ooh* and *ahh* at the miracle of fountains where no rain falls. Rather than steward and care for the oases nature gave us, we bask in the poolside shade of transplanted palms. Who among us doesn't? We prefer efficiency to conservation— so say the water authorities—because the latter feels punitive.

We want to be free. We want to be distracted. We're the Romans who smile and soak, play low-return games, and laugh when they send in the clowns.

~

MIKE'S FATHER RICHARD WAS BURIED IN A VETERAN'S CEME-
tery outside of Las Vegas. In his final days, Richard had been
reminiscing about his World War II service and may have even
requested the honor guard that he'd earned. He'd flown C-47
supply planes in Burma at the time when airmen were crossing
"The Hump" over the Himalayas from India to China without
navigation systems. Taking inordinate risks, routinely pushing
aircraft rated for eighteen thousand feet another ten thousand
higher, the soft-spoken Richard had been a badass pilot at age
twenty.

Even so, Mike found the military funeral surreal. "There
were the marines and their starched, stiff outfits. They folded
the flag and took it to The Widow, as she was called, and then
saluted her. It reminded me of John F. Kennedy's tribute or
something." Most of Richard's surviving friends were hundreds
of miles away in Los Angeles and too elderly to travel. All the
other attendees were Annie's family and friends. Of the elegies
read, only Mike's described a Richard from a different time and
place. "I concentrated on the father I knew growing up."

Richard's resting place lacks anything wet. "It's very modern, with flat plaques right on the ground. There aren't grave-
stones or anything. There are just markers on concrete and no
greenery anywhere. And it's 110 degrees." Not the emerald
fields of Arlington or Golden Gate National Cemetery. Richard
probably hadn't dared to hope for a long life in those heady
days of transporting explosives over too-high mountain passes
guided only by the sun and stars. Now his gravesite roasts under
unrelenting sun, at a concrete cemetery that he wouldn't have
chosen on a bet, had he been a gambling man.

As Mike was leaving Las Vegas, he helped a friend of
Annie's with her bags at the airport. "Jean and I were standing
in line outside the terminal when a taxi pulled to the curb. A

woman literally fell out of the car. She was dolled up, but her makeup was all streaked. She'd obviously stayed up all night gambling. I've never seen anyone so drunk in my life." The woman cut in front of Mike and Jean in line. "Jean spoke up, saying that we'd been at a funeral. The drunk started swearing and bitching. 'I don't give a fuck about your funeral, I've had a really bad week.' I realized that she'd probably lost everything gambling. And this whole scene just summed up the sadness of the place. That really capped it for me. Farewell to Vegas."

Mike hasn't been back. "Vegas is supposed to be this big, decadent party place, but it's so depressing. People like this drunk woman go home broke. It's not like anybody's really having fun."

He lost touch with Annie, who worked quickly to consolidate her husband's multi-million dollar estate. Mike did consult with a lawyer and had asked his father in earlier years about some valuable family properties that predated Annie and even Richard. In the end, though, Mike's soft-spoken accountant father either failed to act or did so passively: he didn't write a will or trust. All his wealth went to Annie—or rather to Las Vegas, where she now lives and, Mike believes, gambles. Her short jaunts to the escape of an adult playground became one long trip.

He is mostly contemplative about it. "She was always so meek and nervous around me, but clearly she had this other side. She wanted to be treated like a queen, in the casino's VIP lines and such. They're just these phony preferences, though, and she can't see through it."

Mike grieves his father and his strange end. "What's awful is that Dad's soul has to bake in a hell like that. But there he is."

AND THERE WE FOUR KIDS WERE, IN A LAS VEGAS ALLEY WITH our folks, coming closer to an ill-dressed clown sweeping concrete. Panic grew in me. Clearly we wouldn't be getting away without at least making eye contact. He saw the six of us and stopped working. My skin prickled with caution. Nevertheless we all gathered around this man who looked nothing like Bozo or Ronald but instead like the itinerant men we'd seen in train-yards, raggedy transients our family had dubbed "H. O. Boes." The word *homeless* hadn't yet entered our vocabulary.

My ever-outgoing father asked him, "Aren't you Emmett Kelly?"

"I am." The clown leaned on his broom and took us all in. His eyes sparkled from a face coated in makeup.

My father and Mr. Kelly shook hands like old friends. In a way, they were. Dad had known of Emmett Kelly Sr.'s circus acts in the thirties. He'd even seen Mr. Kelly's character Weary Willie play for laughs at a time when they were as rare as hundred dollar bills. An *existential clown*, or *tramp clown* like Buster Keaton and Charlie Chaplin, Mr. Kelly Sr. had worked hard or hardly worked, did his best against entire armies, found beauty in fragile garden flowers. He often got the girl, even dressed in an arguably unattractive way: white lips to accentuate a frown, ashen whiskers, clothing that might've been fished out of a dumpster. And pushing a broom? Just part of the king-of-the-road lifestyle.

The clown in the alley, I learned later, was Emmett Kelly Jr., the son of the original. Either one would have been as big a celebrity as I'd ever met. At that moment, though, Mr. Kelly Jr. seemed like a regular guy. He'd been acting the janitor, and I knew at least one other like him—the custodian at my school—a man in the realm of the real. Mr. Kelly Jr. was in costume, but not in character. He turned a genuine spotlight of attention upon us for the few minutes we spoke. He wasn't responsible for this fake-o town. He only worked here.

He warned us kids to "stay away from places like this." He handed out postcards, signed with a fountain pen, according to my younger brother, who remembers everything.

When I reported to my third-grade class about My Spring Break in the Desert, I mentioned the ethereal beauty of the Grand Canyon. The painted movie sets in Old Tucson. The horses we'd ridden up a dry wash in Wickenburg—a rural landscape that felt to me like wilderness. I wowed my peers with talk of a mountain lion I'd seen, even though it lived behind glass at the Arizona-Sonora Desert Museum. No one questioned any of these fantastical events until I mentioned Las Vegas and meeting a famous clown.

"Emmett Kelly was sweeping an alley?" my teacher asked. She didn't say anything more, but her reproachful look spoke plenty.

I held up a postcard, evidence that I'd seen him. I didn't have the words, though, to convey that he'd been working with the care of someone whose job it was to clean up after a show. At the moment of our meeting, he was no more part of an act than my family. Among artificial lights in a growing faux oasis, fed by elaborate waterworks irrigating a stopover in the desert where the ecotone was being turned to toast, Mr. Kelly Jr. was the real deal. He knew his craft by heart, learned from his father before him. He played his role alongside that old shapeshifter water, which poured through fountains and canals and sprinklers and spas to nourish the Las Vegas sleight of hand: let me separate you from your purse. He, however, was authentic to the core—as real as the river harnessed to liven the adult playground. As real as Mike's father, the World War II pilot who is buried there.

I could tell. I was still a kid. I'd have known a phony when I saw one.

3.

SEVENTEEN PALMS

J IM DICE PHONES AS SOON AS HE GETS MY EMAIL. HIS VOICE
is urgent. He's just read my proposal to study the connection
between palm oases and declining groundwater near the town
of Borrego Springs, where he lives. "Palms grow in spring-fed
canyons," he says, "mostly along fractures and faults, where they're
still getting good water." He thinks I might not see immediate
visual evidence of a falling water table on the palms in his area.
Jim knows his business, so I take note. He was a ranger and
resource manager in Anza-Borrego Desert State Park; now
he's the first reserve manager of UC Irvine's Steele/Burnand
Anza-Borrego Desert Research Center. He talks to visiting
biologists, geologists, paleontologists, and anthropologists, some
of whom come to the community for research and never leave.
He's explored most of the region. His laidback style disguises a
fierce intellect and encyclopedic knowledge of the desert.

Mid-conversation, Jim pauses to consider. "But some mesquite groves have died off from lack of water. And Seventeen
Palms, one of the oases, did dry up."

Seventeen Palms: rather than a narrow-canyon refuge, with
tumbling falls and riparian plants like willows and sedges, it's
an exposed stand of palms in a wide arroyo near the park's badlands. A longtime docent at the state park visitor center tells
me it's his favorite grove. "It's not hidden up hard-to-climb

canyons like most palm groves around here. It's standing right out in the middle of nowhere. You just come around the corner, and there it is." His description rings a bell in my memory. On Christmas Eve in 2003, I traveled to Seventeen Palms with eleven relatives ranging in age from four to eighty. We drove three cars into Arroyo Salado on a soft, dirt road. Crumbling alluvial bluffs stood on either side of us, blocking vistas and providing the singular isolation that comes with dropping below the horizon. The arroyo is only safely negotiated in four-wheel-drive vehicles, and still it's a fishtailing, potentially high-centering experience. We dodged all the dangers, going at a conservative pace, reaching a packed-down parking area around noon. From there we hiked a short distance over the bald canyon floor with our lunch in coolers and grocery sacks. On a sandy slope safely away from the palms' network of roots, we set up a picnic.

Like the Oasis of Mara, Seventeen Palms has no central pool of standing water or ring of supporting desert plants. It's simply a few clusters of palms in a wide canyon aligned northwest-southeast and aimed at the corrugated Santa Rosa Mountains. A jumble of fallen fronds hides a spring, invisible but for a wooden sign warning, *Not for Cooking or Drinking*. Camping is prohibited to protect the water source for nighttime visits by wildlife. A makeshift "post office" consists of handwritten notes stuffed into a tin can tucked among the trees. Plastic bottles standing nearby hold only a swallow or two of water.

Visitors from older times who'd left notes in this same post office claim to have found the spring drinkable. A century ago, the US Geological Survey deemed the water potable even though best taken only in an emergency. In 1909, geologist W. C. Mendenhall wrote, "When the spring is kept open, the water is fairly good, but it becomes bitter and bad from disuse. The soil is impregnated with alkaline and salts." Hence the canyon's name *Arroyo Salado*, or "salty gulch."

Nonetheless, native people may have known the spring and used it. The region around Seventeen Palms drew cross-country foot traffic of prehistoric people, Cahuilla who lived north of the oasis and Kumeyaay who lived south. Archaeologists say the most intensive times of indigenous occupation near present-day Anza-Borrego Desert State Park were about 1,100 years ago and then again 800 years later (310 to 360 years before today). Numerous trails throughout the Colorado Desert still show the routes along which wide-ranging, food-gathering forays and extensive trade networking occurred. Paths wind into the hills and then down to the desert floor, where people were drawn during inclement seasons.

Similarly, my family finished our Christmas Eve lunch in the protection of a sandy wash, at Seventeen Palms oasis. My brothers entertained us with a skit they'd learned at Boy Scout camp (one of the more innocent acts, they claimed). My older brother walked on all fours portraying a mule while my younger brother, playing the animal's prospector-owner, snapped a fallen palm frond over its head. "Patience, jackass, patience," the cruel owner said, more times than I can remember.

They circled outside the clusters of trees, the "mule" begging for water over and over while his owner denied him. This scenario repeated for many minutes until my eighty-year-old father asked when something was going to happen. To which my brothers answered in unison, "Patience, jackass, patience," amusing everyone, especially the teenagers.

THE FIRST THING TO KNOW ABOUT SEVENTEEN PALMS—OR about many groves of California fan palms, for that matter—is that it does not contain the exact number of trees in its name. As in the Oasis of Mara outside Twentynine Palms, the trees come and go, thinned by fire, flood, old age, and compaction of their roots by visitors. The numerical names of groves, though, tend to stick despite their inaccuracy. Seventeen Palms has been called that since the late 1800s, when the eponymous palm count occurred. Later, in 1918, author J. Smeaton Chase camped at the spring and counted "six or eight" trees. Whether Smeaton was counting by moonlight and under the influence of strong drink may not be known, but by the 1940s, reputable sources reported twenty-five palms, some burned.

Today, by my count, twenty-nine palms grow in Seventeen Palms. One of the twenty-nine is really a snag, but it's still standing, so I include it in my tally. I see why grove size is easy to misrepresent, given the numerous palm pups hiding under their parents' skirts. Some counters have simply thrown up their hands and made estimates—or not even that. The town of Twentynine Palms, for instance, is said by local websites to have "too many palms to count."

Too many palms. On a longer timeline, an overabundance of palms would have been apparent in the area. In Pliocene times, 3.5 million years ago, groves grew throughout the state park's modern footprint, following the retreat of an inland ocean called the Imperial Sea. Fossilized wood specimens recently discovered in the region are dead ringers for today's native *Washingtonia*. The trees belonged to an ancient flora on an old Colorado River delta that included ash, buckeye, cottonwood, willow, walnut, avocado, and bay laurel. Some of the plant species survive today, holdovers from the wetter floodplain, which had a fauna that included mammoths and early horses, now extinct. Low-lying streams running to tidal beaches of the day provided plenty of water for thirsty palms, with their fanned, evaporative foliage and barely buried, spreading roots.

Some sixty million years ago, *Washingtonia* lived as far north as Colorado and Wyoming. Today the native palm's natural range doesn't extend beyond southern California, Nevada, Arizona, and Mexico. California's groves tend to cluster at springs along the San Andreas Fault Zone and its many associated smaller rifts. In the Anza-Borrego Desert, faults run northwest-southeast through the park and environs, continuing southward along the Salton Trough.

The faulting is part of seismic forces that separate Baja California from mainland Mexico. The mountains and badlands of the region, including Arroyo Salado, align with the trend of the San Andreas along the west coast of North America. On land, under the desert's surface alluvium, water seeps from associated fractures in wet zones that support groves like Seventeen Palms. Trees may look like they're in "the middle of nowhere," but they're really rooted in moist, hidden faults and fractures in creased hills. Sandy, sometimes-wet washes align with zones of seismicity and other fault-driven landforms.

Seventeen Palms, if it stands in the middle of anything, stands in the middle of geology.

CONTRARY TO LOCAL CUSTOM, I PLAN TO HIKE TO SEVENTEEN Palms. Most visitors don't walk into Arroyo Salado. Most take all-wheel-drive vehicles down it, as we did at Christmas. The "corner" described by the docent at the visitor center is the intersection of the big, wide-open arroyo with a tributary canyon, in a confluence of sloping washes. The rugged, southeast corner of the park consists of gray, rumpled badlands that fall away toward the horizon. To the north, the snow-draped Santa Rosa Mountains rise between Borrego Springs and Palm Springs. At night, the glow of that bigger, better-known community glows beyond peaks that otherwise resemble black holes in a star-glazed sky.

Few visitors stop at Seventeen Palms. Drivers shoot on past, eyes glittering as if winning a rally. They pass even an alluring, tiny hillside grove called Five Palms, as impossible a cluster of trees as one can imagine. The motorists' destination: Ocotillo Wells State Vehicular Recreation Area. Pods of grinning recreationists zoom into the arroyo on their way to the recreation area and zoom out on their way back.

The hiking is easy going except for the insistent tug of soft sand on my boots. It's a lot like beach walking. Last night one of the season's Pacific storms, driven by El Niño, scoured the arroyo clean of tire tracks and washed fans of light-gray sand over the older, darker channel bottom. Fresh rockfalls and calving cliffs have tumbled onto the road. The storm also closed Highway 101 near Santa Barbara with the mudslides and flooding perennial to the coast. This morning, in Borrego Springs, temporary signs standing in roadways warned of flooding. Knee-deep waters had filled certain streets the prior afternoon but had since receded. Spectacular, brown standing waves had come on with little warning and vanished just as fast. Events not to be missed, although they almost always are.

Even on a winter hike, the sun shows no mercy. Hat and dark glasses are *de rigueur* any time of year. Generous, fresh sand lobes catch the sunlight with a granitic gleam. Features that I'm sure I'd have overlooked by car attract my eye. Phainopeplas, black desert birds with jay-like topknots, whistle and fly from branch to branch in the scant scrub. Blossoms of coyote tracks surround pockets of mud that remain from the storm. Creosote waxes pungent in the growing heat. How many birds' nests do I see among the branches of mesquite and smoke trees? More than I'd have thought possible given the lack of water.

Two vehicles that passed me at the beginning of my hike roar through the other way, one chasing the other, both drivers beaming as if shooting easy prey.

THESE DAYS I SUSPECT THAT THE VACATIONS OF MY YOUTH were as much benefit to my parents, who planned and carried them out, as they were to us kids who went along for the ride. The Anza-Borrego Desert, with its fascinating, prickly plant life and packs of keening coyotes, soothes the soul I never know aches until I get back there. My parents must have needed this place, too—their enthusiasm didn't flag for making return trips, with a bunch of four grade-schoolers. They'd pull us out of classes days early so we could make the long drive down two states, much slower going back then, and still enjoy a full week away.

Our teachers loaded us down with extra assignments, but it barely mattered. That additional work just meant after-breakfast sessions at campsite picnic tables with my father overseeing math problems on the order of $4 + 5 = 9$ and $3 + 10 = 13$. Those easy additions have their eerie equivalents today in computer authentication tests that ask whether I'm human. In those days I never doubted that I was, with or without the homework.

Each time we arrived in Borrego Springs, I breathed a sigh of relief to see that it hadn't changed. Somehow I'd inherited my parents' wish that it never become Palm Springs. The town stayed small, with the same familiar grocery stores and cafés. And why shouldn't it? It had everything we dreamed of and more: the always-alluring hikes or drives to the skirted groves up Palm, Coyote, and Hellhole Canyons; nighttime campfire programs where good-natured rangers led us in amusing songs about cactus-human interactions and views of the Milky Way; the swimming pool at the old Palms Resort, with its vending machine full of Fantas and Hires and its jukebox of hits like "Ahab the Arab" and "Venus in Blue Jeans."

Even as kids we wanted to always find desert bighorn sheep, roadrunners, century plants in bloom, lost mines, and new barrel cactus that appeared the size of bowling balls following rainstorms that wet the desert floor. The California fan palm remained the icon of it all—that native, prehistoric holdover that managed to be exotic in appearance. How sweet that it represented wetter times right where it stood.

Always, always, we feared the day that our home away from home would be lost. After all, hadn't many places in California gone under the developer's knife? We had a sense that the limiting factor to growth was water, but even back then we'd seen that barrier overcome through elaborate plumbing all over the West. Later, when Las Vegas became an international destination resort even without an unlimited aquifer, and Palm Springs went from ten golf courses to more than 124, then it was certain that Borrego Springs would transmogrify. How could the town stay tiny, located as it was beside a wilderness park where palm trees and desert bighorn sheep were the draw and resorts were also dying for change?

TODAY MY MOTHER HAS BEEN GONE THIRTY YEARS; MY FATHER has reached ninety-five. Just this year he lost his second wife, to whom he was married twenty-nine years. Until he was eighty, he kept the Borrego Springs tradition going—he was the one who issued invitations for annual family peregrinations there. He switched our seasonal trips to winter holidays, turning what might've been dreaded seasonal obligations to longed-for reunions. When he remarried, his new wife became the latest desert devotee. She embraced the campfires, star walks, and day hikes to the oases. When she left us, too, our family's desert dreams became lonelier, held closer to fewer shirts.

Despite his advanced dementia now, and his status as a shut-in, my father smiles when I mention the word *Borrego*. A light turns on in his eyes. When I visit him with old and new photographs of the desert and short movie clips of canyon groves, he turns off the otherwise-constant noise of the television. We admire close-ups of the palms' scaly bark. We flip through pictures of ragged fronds against a blue sky. He guesses where the photos were taken. "Palm Canyon?" or "the visitor center?" With each slide, he hums with recognition. When he sees a picture of a creek bed lined with granite boulders wet from the rains, he says, "This is good. This is really good."

EMILY BROOKS IS AN ENVIRONMENTAL ANTHROPOLOGIST who researches the Western Colorado Desert (the part of the Sonoran Desert that includes the Anza-Borrego). For years, she's been collecting field data on communities living in hostile conditions. Over dinner at Carmelita's, one of Borrego Springs' popular Mexican restaurants, Emily brings me up to speed: seventy percent of local groundwater is pumped for agriculture, twenty for resorts, and ten percent for municipal and ecosystem uses. A 2015 report by the US Geological Survey published these figures. "There may be only twenty years left in the aquifer at current use," Emily says.

She describes the human tendency to overdraw groundwater in the desert as a sort of water hangover. "People still want lawns and swimming pools, but they're facing the end of groundwater. Some don't believe that the big water projects in California are really over. Down near the Salton Sea, people talk about desalination and a pipeline from the coast. They're holding out for something from the outside to save them. You don't hear that so much around the rest of the state anymore." While other Californians discuss conservation and small-scale solutions, the little communities in what Emily calls the "less sexy deserts" like the Anza-Borrego still hope for the bigger fix.

Generational differences have emerged in Emily's data. "Some people moved out to tiny towns all along the border of the state park because they love wilderness or craved the quiet or could afford it out here. Now they've aged in place, and some are stuck. They may live in areas that are potentially environmentally at risk, but they can't afford to move. An entire generation might be facing an end to their community coinciding with the end of their own lives."

Later Emily and I visit Carlee's, a restaurant-bar with drinks named for the desert: Cactus Cooler, Water Hazard, and Flash Flood. One of the town's most popular bands, Elevation 597, is playing covers of popular songs, some contemporary, some dating back to the days when my siblings and I frequented the pool at the Palms Resort. The musicians balance their gigging with day jobs, and Emily knows them all: the lead guitarist is a former park ranger, the lead singer a yoga instructor, the rhythm guitarist a business owner and manager whose voice, his wife confides in us, wows the ladies in town.

Everybody comes to Carlee's. They dance. They eat huge plates of burgers, French fries, and green salads. They sing along to Madonna songs and walk like Egyptians. They're the heart of Borrego Springs, where you can just be yourself.

To me they're the ten percenters, the small fraction of municipal and ecosystem water users. Like the desert bighorn sheep (*borregos* in Spanish) for whom the place is named, like the hummingbirds who frequent the crimson ocotillo blooms, like the snowbirds who flock here from Washington state and British Columbia, many have come because they love the desert for what it is. They aren't here to golf. They aren't here to buy acreage for grapefruit production. They're here to bird-watch, cycle, count desert bighorn sheep, stargaze, and hike to palm oases.

The ten percenters are farmworkers. Groundskeepers. Receptionists. Managers. Chefs. Bellboys. Desk clerks. Similarly the wildlife community—also ten percenters—relies on groundwater that is being pumped to depletion by those who control the biggest withdrawals. The survival of the ten percenters is not in their own hands. Even more, their lifestyles, dependent on water, won't continue unchanged until the moment the aquifer vanishes. "This community won't survive the way it has until the water dries up," Emily says. "Before that happens, we'll be seeing the end of a way of life."

"THERE'S NOTHING HERE." SO I OVERHEAR A CUSTOMER SAY AT one of two grocery stores in Borrego Springs. There's nothing but empty acres of wild desert and dark night skies. It's precisely that nothingness that brings me here again and again. The last time I visited town with my whole family, including my father and stepmother, we stayed as usual at the Oasis Motel on the outskirts of town. The motel has six guest rooms in a building of cinder-block construction. An outdoor whirlpool allows excellent views of craggy Indian Head Peak jutting into the wide sky from the San Jacinto Mountains. Old, louvered windows help motel guests stay connected to the desert just by keeping their glass slats at horizontal. At the Oasis, I used to stay up late reading Sam Shepard plays about the West—grim family dramas in which howling coyotes served as a motif for desolation. Outside the motel, real packs of coyotes wailed into the night.

Borrego Springs' population has remained small, despite periodic attempts by promoters to attract more residents and visitors. By 2010 the US Census Bureau cited the population of the Springs as 3,400, up approximately 1,000 residents since the year 2000. A big boost, but still small for California, and minute for a potential resort destination only sixty miles north of San Diego. The town has a relaxed, intermittent flow of vehicle traffic around a small, grassy park called Christmas Circle. Old-fashioned services and a quirky, sometimes-open movie theater don't tend to attract upscale visitors. There's nothing here but an iconoclastic community and surrounding wilderness with half the real estate of California's entire state park holdings.

Borrego Springs remains Borrego Springs, at least to the naked eye. It's what you can't see that has changed, and it's significant: the town has relied solely on groundwater sources for drinking water and irrigation since the valley was first settled. Borrego Valley is not on The Pipe—one iconic name for the infrastructure that imports water from the Colorado River—and so cannot slake its over-allocations as other cities in the West have done (Las Vegas, Los Angeles, Santa Barbara).

Borrego Springs has withdrawn more groundwater than can recharge naturally from its scant annual rainfall. In its overdrafts, Borrego Springs is not alone—pumping groundwater is a common strategy that allows agriculture, recreation, and municipal functions to coexist on arid lands in the West. The 2015 US Geological Survey report referred to by Emily Brooks summarized the many groundwater studies that have been conducted in Borrego Valley since the early 1900s. The review of research also brought the state of science up to date. In a climate that has averaged less than six inches of rain per year since 1942, new recharge to groundwater supplies is slow, approximately 5,600 acre-feet annually. (One acre-foot equals one acre one foot deep in water, which equals approximately 326,000 gallons.) The 20,000 acre-feet drawn from the subsurface under Borrego Springs every year has dropped the water table in some parts of the valley as much as 100 feet. Such extensive pumping has drawn unwanted minerals such as arsenic into water-supply wells from the surrounding soil and rock. Other wells have dried up.

In a way, the visitor in the grocery store is right, there's nothing here—nothing but decline and challenge and poignancy over a puzzle that hasn't been solved.

After hiking to Seventeen Palms, I continue to Five Palms, which may actually contain only five palms. Again, it's not easy to tell, given a dense understory of palm skirts that cover growth near the ground. Palm pups the size of tabletop Christmas trees can hide there, among the fronds of their elders. Although neither Seventeen Palms nor Five Palms has an open-water hydric zone, they do offer solace and shade to wildlife and other travelers in this remote part of the park. Those aspects of an oasis are much needed. Something about the groves surviving on arid hill-slopes and in wide, sun-drenched washes captures the imagination, too, appealing endlessly to desert rats like the longtime park docent. And my family.

I sit in the shade cast onto a hillside by the trunks of five palms. Two SUVs creep down the wash and, after passing Five Palms, back up to park at its trailhead. Each SUV carries a driver and his passenger. Someone rolls down a window, holds a cell phone outside the cab, snaps a photo. I don't think they see me. I'm kind of hidden behind the ridiculously small oasis. They drive on toward the badlands proper.

These isolated oases will remain here through the grace of God and groundwater, the latter creeping along fault systems that slice the land. Sometimes there is enough water for the palms, and they hang on. The choices the Borrego Springs citizens face about how to use groundwater are theirs to make, yes, but the consequences are not theirs alone to suffer. As their aquifer fares, as their groundwater goes, so go the oases. So go the desert rats who come from all over the world to love the place. So goes the wildlife who live here and depend more and more on land managers to irrigate and construct water guzzlers where springs have dried up.

Here in Arroyo Salado, and all over the Anza-Borrego Desert, there's some version of my brothers' "Patience, jackass, patience" skit going on. Like the attenuated ending of their playacting, like the conclusion my father wanted them to get to when they wouldn't do it themselves, there's something in the Borrego Springs water picture that resembles an inevitable ending delayed past its time. Whether failing to adopt good water stewardship is passive-aggressive, like the jackass skit, or just passive, it's certainly evidence of lack of will. As I hike and love the desert, I can't fathom where that love will go when these arid places lose the oases that make them habitable.

4.

A LOT TO LEARN

M Y FIRST AND LONGEST-TERM LOVE AFFAIR BEGAN, AS many great loves do, on a perfect summer day beside a shining body of water. I was seventeen. Within months of discovering the object of my affection, the Stanislaus River, I learned to guide there. It was a lovely Sierra Nevada stream, the ideal place to learn the art and science of running whitewater. On my first trip, though, before I'd ever considered becoming a rafter myself, I found a band of men and women who'd already made the Stan their spiritual home. They'd been goners for the river for years: its energized currents and quiet places, its deep eddies and standing waves. They loved the rock walls ringing with calls of canyon wrens. Their hearts beat faster to see but-terflies dancing by on breezes, as if choreographed. The shade of canopied trees became their shelter. The river soothed and seduced and healed.

That year I discovered, too—in a one-two punch—the knockdown, drag-out side of love. The stretch of river I'd just fallen for was doomed, planned for submersion under its own collected waters behind an earth-fill dam. The new feat of engineering would be called New Melones—such an innoc-uous name, Spanish for *melons*. The dam would be sited, as so many before it in California had been, atop the location of an historic town of the same name. Reputedly christened for the gourd-shaped and -sized gold nuggets mined there during the 1840s, the settlement of Melones, too, was doomed. It now lives mainly on registers of permanently destroyed towns. Not ghost towns, which still stand at least in part, but towns wiped off the Earth.

Destroyed towns in California didn't suffer the same types of demise seen in other parts of the world—destruction by the Luftwaffe, for instance, or raiding by the Greek army. Rather, the lost communities in California were taken out by feats of engineering. One list that accounts for fifty-three destroyed towns around the world includes twenty-seven in California; of those, all but one were historic, streamside communities inundated by reservoirs. The twenty-eighth, Silsbee, sank beneath an overflow of the Colorado River diverted to the Imperial Valley for irrigation. Same difference.

The list of fifty-three would swell larger by far if it included the countless Native American villages that preceded European presence: the shady, sand-and-bedrock settlements of prehistoric people that disappeared under the same dam-related floods. Those dwelling places weren't evident in old buildings, foundations, and barns; rather, they were found in the curved bowls of meal-grinding rocks, footpaths that wound along stream shores, shards of obsidian and clay. The people who'd lived and breathed and raised their children for millennia along California's foothill rivers were known as *Pohonichi* or Southern Sierra Miwok, *Monachi* or Western Mono, *Inyana* or Upper Kings-Kaweah River Yokoch (also called Yokut)—and many more family bands, too many to count. Oral histories tell us that one hundred people or so gathered in each settlement. The memory of their beloved places slipped under water along with the rest.

DURING MY FIRST TRIP ON THE STAN IN 1972, THE TOWN OF Melones was still there. A dam already stood upstream of it, serving the stately functions of water storage and flood control. In the existing reservoir, the type of recreation promised for the new dam—lake boating and water skiing and navel gazing—was happily going on. Old Melones Lake didn't disturb the town, and it preserved the historic and prehistoric features and natural beauty that so many loved, just upstream. The screamingly popular eighteen-mile rafting run, also upstream, brought positive economic impact to the area, as did the old town. River runners and lake boaters alike loved to explore the quaint, historic communities of Melones, Jamestown, Sonora, and Angel's Camp.

But New Melones Dam was *needed*. It was on the books. It would serve the growing water and power appetites of Californians. Its projected benefits would help meet a future in which clean, hydroelectric power generation would constitute an important component of California's energy portfolio.

THOSE OF US WHO LOVED THE RIVER BELIEVED WITH SHINING confidence that the Bureau of Reclamation's plan for the Stan was all a mistake. Joining the drive for signatures on a petition, I worked alongside others who also had the fervent dedication of the newly indoctrinated. We set up signing tables in Sacramento, in the San Francisco Bay Area, in little gold towns throughout the Sierra foothills, and at the river's edge. We were used to living on the river as guides, and now we did more of it to rescue the river. We were on a crusade.

Few people, when approached, refused to sign. Those who did often changed their minds when we explained that a signature simply helped to put a referendum on the ballot. Finding it harmless enough, doubters would acquiesce, scribble their signatures, and hurry away, perhaps feeling just a little roped in. Few stuck around to converse.

On rafting trips, we kept petitions ready in our ammo boxes. Guests fresh off of river trips tended to be enthusiastic signers. The power of moving water still held them like a magic spell—they not only didn't want to leave the wild river, they had become its advocate. "Just tell me where to sign," they said, at swimming beaches, rocky bars, and shady campsites. Riverside boulders served as perfect perches for the converted to hold clipboards in their laps and scribble their names and addresses.

In that environment, few people balked at signing, although my memory retains the face of one outspoken fellow. He'd just spent the day plunging through whitewater, delighting at the rush of rapids, and water-fighting. He'd joined all the fun with the ferocity of someone with a big heart.

At take-out, he showed off his convertible sedan, driving it close to the rafts that we guides were cleaning and deflating. Presumably he wanted us to see him looking good in it. Imagine my surprise when I saw our lead guide riding with him. She was a beautiful blond woman with a winning smile and knack for schmoozing. They'd apparently been off somewhere private and now were back.

I wasn't the only one surprised by their quasi-pairing. The lead guide's boyfriend, a sweet-natured, long-haired assistant who played guitar and always smiled, had been helping with the rafts and working hard as usual. When he saw her with the convertible driver, a rare cloud crossed his face. He and I met eyes. He shook his head and went back to de-rigging.

The convertible guy and the lead guide walked around looking elated, all smiles. I sensed his bliss and used the moment to approach him with a petition and clipboard.

"I don't think so, love," he said, in a brogue or burr or whatever he had. Clearly he wasn't American, which made him at least a little attractive. "I don't like to back a losing team."

A quick trembling came over me, out of fear, or anger, or both, but I surprised myself by saying, "So sign it anyway. If we can't save the Stanislaus, maybe we'll somehow save another river, like the Tuolumne, which could be next."

I don't know where I'd heard that argument. Maybe it was my own. The sense that the Tuolumne River could be dammed further than it already had been, which was pretty much to the teeth, was no big stretch. In fact, a fight would follow, years later: a proposed dam at the confluence of the Tuolumne with the Clavey, another bad idea that pitched another passionate fight. At that moment, though, I was simply pulling a long-eared rodent from a hat.

The convertible guy looked at me as if I'd just come into focus. He took my petition in one hand and my pen in the other. Without setting down the cigarette he'd been smoking, resting the clipboard on the lead guide's peachy, bare shoulder, he wrote his name on one of the many signatory lines.

I walked away feeling both sheepish for pushing him and victorious for having succeeded.

RECENTLY, CONSTRUCTION BEGAN ON WHAT'S KNOWN AS SITE C, the third in a string of dams on the Peace River in northeast British Columbia. The pastoral Peace, a twelve-hundred-mile-long stream, originates in the Rocky Mountains and goes on to flow through northern Alberta's flat-lying, glaciated, wheat-growing country. The region has fertile soil, abundant cultural sites, rich prehistory and history, and communities that, frankly, don't want a dam. According to BC Hydro, the utility behind Site C, the Peace's newest reservoir will be the second coming. The dam will produce "thirty-five per cent of the energy" of the two existing projects, using "only five per cent of the reservoir area." Once completed, Site C "will be a source of clean, reliable, and affordable electricity in BC for more than one hundred years." So says the company that's being paid very well to build it.

Dams have long been touted as green, multiple-use projects. They have roots in the big-dam era of the early to mid

1900s, when engineering feats like Hoover and Grand Coulee promised clean power generation, flood control, and water storage. Site C follows in that same tradition of assurances, even vowing job creation and benefits for First Nations people among the project's dividends.

Yet opposition to Site C has been strong for years. The Prophet River and West Moberly First Nations people of British Columbia, living on lands signed into treaty on June 21, 1899, by Queen Victoria of England, are among the most vocal opponents. They may not live within the planned flood zone, but they've long hunted, fished, trapped, and gathered berries and plant medicines there. Bears and eagles are sought locally for cultural reasons. The Peace floodplain is prime moose-hunting habitat, too. At the Site C Community Input Sessions in 2017, a commenter noted that, among other impacts, Site C would flood a series of small islands where moose take shelter when calving. The commenter, anonymously quoted in the public input section of the "British Columbia Utilities Commission Inquiry Respecting Site C," also said, "[E]lder Lillian Gauthier says she could live without electric lights and a fridge, but she'd be lost if her family could no longer hunt moose."

Although the Canadian government has voiced a commitment to reconciliation for historical wrongs to First Nations people, little has been done to back the pledge. There has been no meaningful consultation with First Nations on Site C—as is common for hydro projects, comments are recorded only to be argued away. On this concern alone, the United Nations has recommended that dam construction be canceled.

IF WE'VE LEARNED ANYTHING FROM THE PAST, INCLUDING from the bitter 1970s battle over New Melones in California, it's that we all, particularly indigenous people, have good reason to be wary of promises made about dams. New Melones was designed to replace and impound water over the existing Melones Dam three quarters of a mile upstream. Plenty of prehistorically and historically important sites went under with it. Despite our petitioning, and a bitter fight that included protests in cities as well as on riverbanks, dam-building went forward. It covered the beloved whitewater run on the Stanislaus River, where we rafting guides had cut our boating teeth on rapids like Death Rock, Razorback Rapids, and Widow Maker. It covered Miwok pictographs, mining artifacts, wildlife homes and bird nests, and stands of living forest and scrub.

Ironically, the US Department of the Interior Bureau of Reclamation, which pushed the project through, now asks visitors to New Melones reservoir to "help protect historic resources by not handling, removing, or destroying any artifacts or ruins along the lake bed. These sites and artifacts are protected by federal and state laws that prohibit disturbing the sites in any way."

New Melones proved to be as wasteful a project as opponents had predicted.

Outdated before construction even began, the future reservoir was justified on water inflows estimated from 1922 to 1978 rainfall patterns. Models failed to factor in cycles of drought and demand that scientists and engineers *already knew about.* The project went forward anyway, as engineered. It came as no surprise, then, that ensuing power production and water supply missed "by a significant amount," in the Bureau of Reclamation's own, subsequent words. New Melones was significantly overbuilt, too big for its britches. Since its initial filling in 1978, the reservoir has only reached near-capacity five times. On average, New Melones sits forty-three percent full during June and July, its highest-capacity months. In 2016, the fifth year of "hot drought"—the hottest and driest spell in California since record-keeping began in the 1800s—the reservoir was just twenty-seven percent full. Without the water hoped for, prayed for, and figured into equations, the storage that the older dam had provided would've been plenty.

New Melones had been authorized in 1944 under the Central Valley Project. Back then the Bureau had been optimistic, pre-selling contracts for irrigation. Those promises on paper now are not met. Drought conditions beginning in 1994 forced the Bureau to make expensive purchases of water from older dam projects to meet its commitments. "It is believed that New Melones does not have a sustainable water supply sufficient to meet existing obligations for irrigation, wildlife enhancement, and water quality improvement," the Bureau notes on its New Melones project history webpage.

Power generation has been under-delivered at New Melones as well, due to lack of in- and outflow. In that regard, it's no different from other hydroelectric power plants statewide. In the hot drought, California's hydroelectricity capability in 2014 had already fallen to twelve percent of total electrical generation from the eighteen percent that it had managed to maintain in dry, superheated 2012. Energy production in the dry years became more costly by roughly $1.2 billion.

Given the history of New Melones, Site C, too, promises to under-perform. The North American Drought Monitor shows British Columbia to be increasingly, abnormally dry, with severe, long-term drought becoming more common in many areas. The great northern forest isn't as wet or cool as it needs to be to support Site C, not anymore. In addition, dams are proving to be huge contributors to the very global warming that renders them obsolete. Vincent St. Louis, a biogeochemist at the University of Alberta, Edmonton, was lead author of a *BioScience* paper in 2000 that was the first to gauge global emissions from reservoirs. "Methane's the story," Vincent told *Science* in 2016. The production of methane by submerged microbes living on organic material that settles with sediment in reservoirs contributes significantly to the suite of greenhouse gases raising global temperatures. In short, dams aren't the clean energy source they're chalked up to be.

Available climate models project multiple scenarios for dams, none of which show up accurately in public relations materials. That's the way of *spin*, though—it's both a "particular bias, interpretation, or point of view" and a "fast, revolving descent." Biased storytelling is not easy to counter once begun, but the truth emerges, as it has with New Melones. The dam's name, so inauspicious at first glance, has a second, salacious meaning; per the good old *Oxford English Dictionary*, *melon* can mean "a large profit, especially one divided among a number of people." In the case of the Stanislaus River, the slicing up of its ripe, sweet globe of fruit evoked an old label for government projects designed to enrich certain districts, legislators, and contractors: *pork barrel*. One slice for the Bureau, one for the builders, one for the backers, one for politicians. None for forest and wildlife, none for the river, none for local communities, not much for you and me.

THE MAN WITH THE CONVERTIBLE EVENTUALLY DROVE UP the rutted dirt road from the Stanislaus takeout, without our lead guide. When he'd gone, I confronted her about hanging out with a guy like that, right in front of her devoted boyfriend. What was she thinking? Wasn't the convertible guy married? My parents had raised me with an old-fashioned, New England sensibility that assigned faithfulness to marriage. I still operated under that assumption.

The lead guide threw back her golden head and laughed. "I'm married, too," she said.

"To him?" I aimed a thumb at the long-haired boyfriend.

No. The boyfriend had been after her to finalize her divorce, but she wasn't in a hurry. She changed the subject to how lucky the river was to have me on its side. My extracting a signature out of her beau-for-the-day had impressed her. "You came up with a good one when he wasn't going to sign. You're really quick. But, about relationships, you have a lot to learn."

I didn't say that I hoped I never learned it.

THE BUREAU AND ITS PROJECT PROPONENTS PUSHED NEW Melones forward with closed ears, eyes, and hearts. Their minds turned away from what was happening all around them, not only in political climate but in weather climate. They couldn't acknowledge that things had changed since 1944. A new world was growing up. Wild places weren't just there to be tamed, but to be known for their restorative beauty. Science had to be relevant; the old ways had to be challenged. Now even the Bureau admits that the controversy surrounding New Melones was a signal that the big-dam era was over.

River guides returned to New Melones to bear witness. Trying to find the deep, green oasis of our youth, though, only serves to prove it's no longer there. Jeffe Aronson writes of returning to the reservoir after it had been filled the first time. The small towns near the river hadn't fared well, with the promised boon to the economy declining as soon as heavy equipment was hauled to the next job. When Jeffe stopped in Angels Camp to look in the empty window of an abandoned market where he used to supply river trips, he felt a tap on his shoulder.

An older gentleman, slightly familiar, smiled and offered his hand. "Aren't you one of those skirt-wearing raft hippies that used to come in back in the 1970s to buy food?" he asked Jeffe. Jeffe admitted that he was, and the man said, "My brother and I used to own this store. We went out of business soon after the dam went in. Whole damn town died. You were right. They lied to us, and I'll regret it for the rest of my life."

DESPITE ALL THE PRECAUTIONARY TALES, SITE C IS GLIDING along in New Melones' slipstream, 1,600 miles to the north. It doesn't take much digging into the facts to understand that the glittering future projected in PR simply won't come true. We have the hard evidence. We now know, for instance, that the costs of deforestation within a new reservoir's footprint equals thirteen dollars per ton of CO_2 no longer sequestered in the trees' roots, trunks, limbs, and leaves. That's pricey. Add that to the tons of methane being produced, and you've got a fortune's worth of greenhouse gases to offset with project benefits. Rivers with salmon fisheries have suffered drastic economic effects following impoundment, devastating communities at the average rate of two thousand dollars per individual salmon lost.

There are downstream impacts, too. For decades, researchers have studied the effects of Glen Canyon Dam on the Colorado River. The dam altered flow regimes so drastically that native fish in the Grand Canyon have died or declined. The impounded river widened in some reaches within the canyon and choked with sediment and debris in others. Challenges for commercial rafters, hugely important to river-related economy, are ongoing. When added to upstream habitat impacts, the monetary values of these and other effects, previously underestimated or not accounted for at all, yield a fortune in environmental costs.

Similarly the price of downstream impacts of the Site C dam remain under-assessed, but they will be exorbitant.

Really, the impacts are priceless. Those who reject the notion of applying a dollar amount to nature know it. First Nations people on the frontlines stand to lose everything integral to their wellbeing: home, way of life, culture, memory, future. They've argued for it, put their lives on the line for it. The potential loss of spiritual and cultural benefits inherent in intact natural habitats cannot be computed.

For these and other reasons, who wouldn't resist Site C? Occupations, hunger strikes, and demonstrations at the river and near the homes and workplaces of decision makers have gone on for years. All are informed by the shortfalls of prior projects. Hundreds of Canadian scholars have petitioned

Prime Minister Trudeau to revisit the plan, in a Statement of Concern pointing out "significant gaps and inadequacies" in regulatory review and environmental assessment. Given new energy and storage options that are emerging, the scholars are right to speak up. Analysts call Site C "fundamentally uneconomic," ready to drain taxpayers of critical funds. BC Hydro's ratepayers will pay in excess of $350 million annually due to outmoded technology and changing energy costs. Not only activists should be outraged about the project.

Most of all, that niggling detail of Canada's increasing aridity hasn't been factored in. Building reservoirs that can only be semi-filled at great dollar and cultural cost—not to mention with huge loss of wildlife- and human-critical habitat—is the same wisdom that destroyed the Stanislaus for no good reason.

"We have plenty of reservoirs that currently aren't full," says Juliet Christian-Smith, a climate specialist with the Union of Concerned Scientists. Smith has suggested that, if anything, preserving groundwater aquifers and storing other water beneath the subsurface is a much smarter and more cost-effective strategy than building more reservoirs, given the warming planet. "Any new storage—whether for groundwater or surface water—must be designed to adapt to the fact that climate change is important to our water-management decisions."

It's time to think smaller. Large dam projects, given the current context, simply don't make sense.

We can meet supply needs by downsizing our approach—particularly given climatic conditions that appear to be the new normal. Sample plans include water reuse, storm-water capture, decentralized systems to minimize energy-intensive transfer costs, indoor and outdoor conservation, and groundwater storage to avoid growing evaporation losses.

∼

Stanislaus guides moved on when the river's doom appeared certain—some to Grand Canyon, as I did, some to other careers. The canyon engaged me completely, as new loves do, but my heart remained bruised over the loss of my first love. Disbelief lingered, with the mix of pain and sweet memory that follows failed romance. Many Grand Canyon guides carried the same wounds I did, those of us who'd apprenticed together on the Stan. We who fled stayed employed as guides elsewhere for years—time that might've been spent on California rivers, had our little gem not gone under. Jeffe Aronson still rows the Grand Canyon commercially, all these years later, but he can't forget the Stan. He regrets abandoning the river that had given him everything, but what else could a guide do?

Who knows where the blond lead guide went, although I did see her once near the town of Santa Cruz, where I attended the university. She was having dinner with yet another sweet boyfriend she'd met on the river; I stopped briefly to chat, then said goodnight. Later I learned they were breaking up right around then. Maybe even that very evening. First the joy and connection, then the loss, then the long, nostalgic future.

Years after being swallowed by its own waters, the Stan again emerged during drought years. Lured by the excitement of media claims that the reservoir was down and the river was back, I kayaked the canyon with my first husband. It was barely runnable—released streamflows were so miniscule that even in such small boats we had to portage much of the four miles that had emerged. Not only that, it was stripped and deadened. Everything not made of rock had been destroyed: gray pines had become standing skeletons, entire hillsides formerly carpeted in wildflowers had gone ashen, willow and alder thickets had turned to black ooze. If a ghost of a river, a murdered thing, excites boaters, then I'm no longer one of them.

Who knows what darkness in the human psyche could allow such a thing? Hard to believe that large-scale reservoir building is seen as making the world a better place. Those who push such projects through must not see the hubris on which they stand—basically, old data and skewed science. To me, and to many besides me, putting a plug in a river is a crime against nature, like depleting groundwater so deeply that the oasis's hydric zone disappears. Who could be blind to the wild and human lives that hang in the balance?

We all have a lot to learn about our relationship to water. We'll never fully get that lesson. Even we who spent our first, sweet, heady days in love with it, by the flowing river, believing it could last forever.

5.

INAPPROPRIATION

ONE OF MY EARLIEST CHILDHOOD MEMORIES IS OF COMING face-to-face with a thicket of blackberry and realizing that I'd wandered into a dead end. I must've turned around to go back home—I don't remember. I do remember that, on that same day, two friends and I found our way across a four-lane highway and to the banks of the Columbia River. My folks hadn't given their consent. Maybe they figured that we'd stay happily playing in our backyard across the river from then-sleepy Portland, as we usually did. On that day, though, we decided to dodge traffic to get across the road and reach the water. It didn't seem like such a big deal to me, but I wasn't yet five years old. I probably wasn't thinking. I was feeling. I wanted more than anything to reach the river, and if I had to cross a highway to get there, so be it.

When we three kids had gotten through the gauntlet of speeding cars and made it to the riverbank, we had our prize: the view. Far down the slope at our feet, the river flexed and gleamed and carried its secrets off into the distance. Later we'd have to stand shoulder to shoulder to face the grownups, but for a moment we had it all. We also found and carried home a speed-limit sign that took all three of us to drag it, but that's another story. This one's about that first view of the river, how it tapped a deep longing that had something to do with living alongside fir and spruce forests and above big rolling waters that were shaping me through no effort of my own.

That sense of what was out there deepened when, as an older grade-schooler, I visited a museum exhibition called *Art of the Northwest Coast*. Unforgettable creature masks and ornate ceremonial tools had been carved and painted by indigenous people and by some miracle—I didn't think it could be thievery—had arrived on the walls before me. The artifacts had labels I could barely interpret and certainly couldn't pronounce—words like *k̲amx'id̲, dzax̲'an̲,* and *x̲al̲a'is*—describing either the materials used in the works or the living things they represented. The aboriginal creations spoke to me with alluring and mysterious voices.

The masks in particular stirred my soul. The carvers of those wooden faces had to be magicians. What was the purpose of the disguises? They had roots in a long-ago time—that was clear to me even as a youth—but I wondered with a wonder that only kids can wonder how much of their tradition lived on. Could such artists be alive and still practicing their craft? If so, where? Certainly not in the proscribed world where one had to brave four lanes of traffic and asphalt to get to a river.

I felt no urge to be a hunter of artifacts or excavator of graves or disturber of ceremonial grounds. I did want to know who in the world made things that could be named *Wood Demon Mask (Haida culture)* and *Three-Quarter Moon Self Portrait (Kwakwaka'wakw)*. The devil I'd seen in picture books didn't have the fantastical, outback look of this demon. Neither had I heard of a person who could claim three-quarters of the moon and call it himself.

A LOVE OF THE CARVINGS NEVER LEFT ME. I FOLLOWED A meandering course of learning and living, out of the Pacific Northwest to the Desert Southwest and East Coast and back to the Pacific Coast, and somehow the catalogue for that first museum show stuck. The catalogue, a glossy paperback book bought with my saved-up allowance, remained in my tiny, moveable collection of permanent references. There was something there that I couldn't express—perhaps nothing more than sweet mystery. Maybe it was the call of wilderness, adventure, lost eras.

Decades later, the same spell of that art seized me when I came upon the much-storied Tlingit Raven helmet used to repel Russian colonizers from Baranof Island, Alaska. During a writing residency with the Island Institute in Sitka, I discovered the helmet at the tiny Sheldon Jackson Museum not far from the Tlingit battleground. The helmet sits in a humidity-controlled glass case at the museum. The wood is worn and no longer painted black. Tufts of fur cling to the crown. The element of disguise is there, though shining in the opaque eyes of the trickster bird. The sturdy beak and head, probably carved of a hardwood burl as Tlingit helmets generally are, were not just for show. Raven had been tested. It had been worn in battle.

The last time had been in autumn 1804, when Chief K'alyaan of the Kiks.ádi Tlingit donned the helmet to protect his homeland (*Shee*, to the Tlingit). Several violent interactions between the native people and the foreign interlopers had led to an attack by the gunboat *Neva* and other ships bearing Russian troops reinforced by Aleut allies. The aggressors landed on stony beaches not far from today's museum. Carrying a blacksmith's hammer, his head covered by Raven and his jaw and throat by a separate shield, K'alyaan and his men went hand-to-hand with the outsiders. After six days of attack and siege, the Tlingit withdrew to the east, some say over the fearsome mountains, some say along the coast. Russian accounts claim that the escapees left small children behind, slain by the Tlingit themselves in their fort near Indian River, outside present-day Sitka. Some called it murder, the work of heartless savages. Others recognized the terrible Hobson's choice the people of the Shee may have made that night. To this day, the Tlingit observe an annual day of mourning for the lives lost in that war.

Now the wood-and-leather reminder of the people's brave defense of home sits in an airless environment. Artists' reproductions of the helmet's former glory show it on K'alyaan's head and face. Raven looks too small to have ever protected any warrior, much less one whose memory is larger than life. But the story lives on in the wood record. Given that the place of honor on totems is at the bottom, not the top as some might think, it's impossible not to feel reverence when standing before master carver Tommy Joseph's K'alyaan Pole commemorating the battle. There, Frog cradles a rendering of Raven in its lap near the ground on which the Tlingit first built a fort, then abandoned it, more than two centuries ago. Other crests of the Kiks.ádi—Beaver, Dog Salmon, Sockeye Salmon, and Woodworm—hold higher, less auspicious places on the pole.

TO CROSS A BORDER INTO ANOTHER COUNTRY IS NO GUARANtee of finding its story. The moment any of us sets foot on new soil, we're beginners. We hear the songs and words of others who've long been there, who have knowledge of every instance of rockfall and changed streambed. With loving familiarity, the native storytellers have described those transient things forever. In the Pacific Northwest of North America, along the coasts of British Columbia and Alaska, the storytellers were also immigrants, arriving in the forests, uplands, and bays from other landmasses, via ocean crossings or over the Bering Land Bridge. The music of the water and wind preceded them; they opened their souls to it. The children of the first immigrants learned through them. Likewise their children's children were born into an openhearted ability to hear.

Europeans who arrived on the West Coast of America ten thousand years later encountered languages as new to them as the still-wild continent. The prior voices were sophisticated, with complicated vocabularies and letters not in the alphabets of the English, Spanish, and French who heard them. The newly arrived didn't understand what was being said, but some wanted to, while the most brutal carried the day. Murder and enslavement ensued while the people sang on, though the music changed, as did their stories, some preserved now only on recordings. We can play them in hushed archival rooms and on the internet, far from the floodplains and coulees and toes of glaciers where they were first told. Those key elements, though, matter as much as the guttural and glottis sounds they rely on for meaning. With the land and water removed, intention is cut out like a still-beating heart.

Their stories are like the Earth's geologic record, where more evidence of time is missing than not. In the case of rock layers, vanishing is caused by erosion by wind, water, and ice. In the case of the original stories, much has been taken through cultural attrition and the work of thugs.

What does endure is resilient—wood, metal, stone. We call it *art*, but the word doesn't begin to describe the mystical, mythical process by which storytellers craft Frog or Raven, Bear or Eagle. The word *art* is static, a result. It hardly describes the life contained within a wooden burl that's strong enough to empower a single individual to face the cannon fire of an invading nation.

In isolated geographies like islands and the most sand-bound oases, water holds all the aces. The Island Institute, which has hosted me and so many other writers in Sitka, knows this. A forward-thinking humanities organization, they've been focusing on community resilience in a place proving to be exceptionally vulnerable to changing climate. When I applied to go there, it was because I wanted to write stories about water among people who lived with it and thought about it every day: as they motored on Sitka Sound to fish, or rode the

Alaska Marine Highway to work as others drive the interstate, or consulted their tide books to decide whether they needed to respond when tsunami warnings sounded. Carolyn Servid and Dorik Mechau (then the Institute co-directors, now senior fellows) approved my application in a matter of days. We'd been gnawing on the same kinds of issues for decades.

Arriving in September, the same month in which Chief K'alyaan's battle took place, I was lent a spectacular home on Thimbleberry Bay south of town. As I sat at the kitchen table day after day typing away on a manuscript of short stories, the rumpled bay waters of greater Sitka Sound moved and breathed and changed hues by the minute. When humpback whales breached or yet another species of migratory bird stopped on a pier right offshore, I'd grab my binoculars. Otherwise I'd sit still and write before venturing out in the afternoon.

During breaks I walked all over the island or toured it with generous neighbors who lived up and down the shore. Bald eagles hung around like vultures on piers. Varied thrushes, so rare back home, perched everywhere throughout the forest like early Halloween decorations. My hosts' strip of beach led to a freshwater stream where salmon spawned and died and drifted back out to the bay. Gulls poked at the still-living fish, tormenting them or observing those in the final throes of expiring. Day after day, one brown bear the size of a camper-van sat in the creek up to his chest, reaching for fish as they passed, holding them to his nose with a big furry paw. He gulped down the good ones and flung away those that failed the sniff test.

In autumn, a sunny day is a rare jewel in Sitka. The town gets an average of eighty-seven inches of rainfall per year and thirty-three inches of snowfall. During my stay, the sun would burst through the leaden overcast for a few hours before disappearing faster than good wine at a feast. Wherever I walked, I always wore full raingear. So much water flowed onshore and off, in the sky and over the ground, I never expected to hear

Sitka residents talk about water conservation. Yet my hosts were concerned about shortages. They asked me to keep my showers short and my laundry loads small to save on water use. Electricity and drinking water are linked on Baranof Island; power comes from small hydroelectric plants trapping high-gradient streams into reservoirs also used for municipal supply. Running too much at the tap means reduced acre-feet for energy generation. Conversely, gobbling power runs precious drinking stores through turbines and down to the sea. Without conservation, the town comes up short in both power and water.

Freshwater supply is so much a concern that it's the focus of studies throughout the region. The University of Alaska, Fairbanks, is researching Sitka's Blue Lake and Green Lake hydropower projects, looking at expected changes in total and seasonal rainfall and snowpack due to climate-related reduction. Even the most wet of towns (like Sitka), ideally located near mountains and rivers, illustrate the Ancient Mariner's dilemma: "Water, water everywhere, nor any drop to drink."

Lack of fresh water also played an early role in Sitka lore. In the 1700s, decades before K'alyaan, Russian explorers were first arriving up and down the Alaska coast. As they boated the bays and inlets and wooded shores, they encountered indigenous cultures who'd been on the ground since the last ice age. The Tlingit of Shee, oceangoing people, thrived on the island's salmon runs, shellfish, halibut, abundant sea mammals, and other good aquatic eats. The Kiks.ádi had heard of the fur-enamored Russians but hadn't had much to do with them—that is, until 1741, when explorer Alexei Chirikov in the *St. Paul* sent a boatload of sailors ashore for water at present-day Sitka. When the men never returned to the mother ship, Chirikov sent a second boatload with the same results. In the days following, a canoe approached the ship but didn't make contact. Chirikov stayed as long as he dared, his food and water stores decimated, then left the fifteen missing men to their presumed fates. Reportedly reluctant to leave, he and his officers nonetheless beat it back to Kamchatka.

Tlingit oral tradition says the men who went ashore "were accepted" into the community. Better the surety of a strange shore, perhaps, than to risk everything on a parched vessel heading back across the Bering.

WATER IN WESTERN STORYTELLING: THE WHITEWATER nightmares recorded in the journals of New York state's John Wesley Powell, who later plotted the taming of the Green and Colorado Rivers that bested him; the soulful desert narratives of Illinois native Mary Austin, whose earnings from writing about a land of little rain helped with caring for her disabled daughter; Wallace Stegner's childhood that began in Iowa but continued through dusty Montana, Saskatchewan, and Utah ("twenty places in eight states and Canada"), with dryland rivers and deserts that inhabited his profound body of writings; Ed Abbey's forswearing his native Pennsylvania in favor of newfound heartlands in Moab, Utah, on the Colorado River, and Llatikcuf, Arizona, in the Sonoran Desert. Western writers of great influence have often been far from their roots. They've observed their adopted landscapes with outsiders' eyes.

A language had preceded theirs, of course. It, too, incorporated water. Its vocabulary survived in durable material that outlasted even the bones of its authors. *Petroglyphs*, or rock writings, and *pictographs*, or painted symbols and words, embellished desert varnish or mineral staining on boulders and cliffs throughout the West. The drawings often showed the way to good springs and hunting grounds. Labyrinthine maps in stone. Numerous desert bighorn sheep and bear etched into manganese scrim. Some glyphs showed routes into remote canyons—remote for modern people, that is. Some graphs depicted antennae and stout-shouldered beings in headdresses such as we of the twenty-first century have never seen. Standing in the shade of a sandstone cliff with our eyes on alien figures, one wonders what visitors inspired such creations.

At heart we're all visiting. The land and water can be interpreted fresh every time, but we're still just responding. In their 1967 classic, *On the Loose*, Renny and Terry Russell describe the canyons and rivers that had claimed their souls:

> Nature might have made Sphinxes in her spare time
> Or Mona Lisa with her left hand, Blindfolded.
> After the first Artist
> Only the copyist.

So we copy the big rivers and wide forests of our childhoods, or our adopted homelands. So, too, the indigenous masks that I saw in my youth took their inspiration from the face of the Earth. What else is there? The nature of our time here and art both prehistoric and modern are inextricably linked. They're part of a neural net that can't be dissociated from the planet where we live.

ON THIMBLEBERRY BAY, I WROTE AND REWROTE SHORT stories I'd drafted from true events in my river-running days. I knew I was working them to death but couldn't stop. The time stretched long from civil twilight to civil twilight—fifteen hours—and I filled it. At night I read murder mysteries by Sitka poet John Straley, kept an ear out for tsunami warnings and the scratchings of brown bears, and basically spooked myself sleepless. In the mornings I'd be grateful for the blessed sunrise that dispelled whatever creepiness I'd imagined. My time there did help further work on a collection of stories on water: embellished river accidents, midnight conversations on streamside beaches, betrayed friendships, lost loves.

Yet I wanted to write something new. Sitka had such richness to offer. A small town with lasting, multicultural roots that went back thousands of years. The city-sized cruise ships that breezed in on favorable tides and instantly doubled the population. Sitka Sound's inlets were joined by rocky whitewater channels where fresh water streamed out of the heart of mountains unconnected to the mainland. Learning of both the water shortages and the abundance of the rainforest, I wanted to add a narrative about Southeast Alaska to my collection. I'd research setting, background, historical characters, and local concerns. Then I'd fictionalize—I'd make something up!

Toward the end of my stay, Carolyn asked to read my new work. She did, and then returned it with questions. Had I talked to anyone about it? If these characters were based on real people, had I asked their permission? I should consult with the local authors and artists—maybe the learned Richard Nelson (Nels), whose books *The Island Within* and other classics were based on decades of living among the people of Alaska. I should meet Tlingit master carver Tommy Joseph, because there was a carver in my story. She could introduce us.

Her concern baffled me. I'd read the work of migrant Western authors forever—look at Powell, Austin, Stegner, and Abbey. Didn't they write about the West like it was theirs? They'd done their research, but no records suggested that they'd asked permission to use their observations in books. The literature was full of celebrated works about Pacific Northwest people written by outsiders like Margaret Craven (*I Heard the Owl Call My Name*) and Gary Snyder (*Myths and Texts*). I'd never read about them asking permission, although perhaps they had. No one had ever asked *my* permission when they wrote about guiding culture, including about me. My embroidering story based on the culture of others was no different. Legend and story belonged to all of us, like the moon and stars. (My emotion in asking these loaded questions and coming to perfunctory conclusions should've been a clue that I needed to go deeper.) Carolyn, in her greater wisdom, reiterated that I should check with experts like Nels and Tommy.

I missed the chance to talk it over with Nels or Tommy or anyone. My time came to a close, and I ferried home. The archives research and historical primary references I'd consulted would have to do.

Years later, when I researched water issues in Alberta for another book, my neighbor and colleague at the University in Edmonton, Hannah McGregor, put it best: appropriation of story from people who have been colonized is about taking power. It's not enough to say that I wasn't personally involved in the original settling, or that as a woman I've lived with oppression, too. Subjugation continues today, on every continent. Cultures with a history of brutalization are simply asking to impart their own wisdom in their own way. It takes work and time and making inroads to honor indigenous sovereignty. Whether a story is copyrighted or not, finding the teller is the right thing to do, and it makes for better storytelling, anyway. Hannah explained this to me patiently, as a parent to a child, and without judgment.

In Alaska, I had "borrowed" icons, symbols, and tradition from the Tlingit to write what I did. I had the best of intentions but didn't follow a respectful protocol. As a result, my short story about Southeast Alaska lacks the authenticity and equity that it would have had if I'd gone deeper. It does capture something about that time, but perhaps at too great a cost to the narrative and the subject. I'd do it differently now.

THERE'S SOMETHING TO BE LEARNED FROM LAND AND WATER, too, about subjugation. Indigenous wisdom knows it. Bertha Grove, Southern Ute tribal leader, once said at a gathering, "Who talks for the water? Did anyone ask the water permission?" Who asks the water before we siphon it or dam it or rob it of wildness? Who has gone to the oasis and asked to use it as our own? Maybe that was the lesson I'd intuited from the masks and icons that had intrigued me beginning in my youth. I sensed with the sense only children can sense that the very continent had been carved into wood. As for *appropriation*, it'd best be called *inappropriation*, or the flagrant assertion of self over land, water, and cultural identity. It matters when we do it to the people. It matters when we do it to the water. No being should have to fight for sovereignty, as Chief K'alyaan did when he took a stand for his right to live on the outer coast of Shee. Same goes for the very streams flowing from the mountains of his homeland.

6.

MAY ALL BEINGS BE STOKED

VANILLA LIGHT FLOODS THE SKY. SUNSET IS AN HOUR OFF among the wooded hills north of San Francisco. The insight meditation center where I'll spend the week is within sensing distance of the ocean but not in view of it. The hills are steep, with slopes more upright here than at my longtime home thirty miles inland. The verticality is courtesy of the San Andreas and related faults running parallel to the edge of the continent. Rock strata rise up, forced by the relentless grind and push of colliding mobile tectonic plates. This is coastal California's version of standing-up country. Here at the meditation center, amidst these signs of a restless earth, statues of the Buddha sit along paths, under bay trees, and in alcoves. The enlightened one can be found in the shadows of narrow, forested valleys. He's tucked along trails that plunge like ski runs, where redwoods cluster in stream creases. He sits in meditative serenity in surprising, hidden places.

The center has its ground rules. Retreatants must stay for the entire week and participate as fully as possible. We don't have to identify as Buddhist to take part, but while here we're asked to try the practices that are offered. For the purposes of training, we'll refrain from killing, stealing, lying, engaging in sexual misconduct, and abusing or misusing intoxicants. We'll conduct ourselves in silence during a rigorous schedule of meditation that begins with a morning bell at 5:45 and continues to 9:30 at night. We've put away our cell phones, computers, other devices—no binge watching or, for that matter, any kind of watching. Neither are we to read or write.

I'm easy with all the rules but that last one. No reading or writing? How else to solve life's puzzles or to clarify my thinking? My reflective hours are usually spent recording thoughts on paper and receiving them likewise. I'm a bit lost on this one. I dwell on it.

Another guideline holds my attention longer than the others: *Although the drought may seem over, we want to continue to support our Earth by reducing daily water consumption and we ask for your assistance with this while on retreat.* Now this is enlightened. In winter, the season when the state's reservoirs aren't drawn down, almost no one in California utters the words *drought* or *water consumption.* Today the state's dams like Shasta and Oroville are at seventy-five percent of maximum—supposedly high, nothing to cause concern. Even our mindful governor doesn't blow the whistle on water use unless circumstances are dire; during the last multi-year period of little precipitation, he didn't declare a state of emergency until we were three years into it. To most, December is a coasting month, before the next year's dry seasons come on again.

It gets me wondering. A quarter of a million people live in this forested, hilly county, which relies in large part on imported water. "On the pipe," Marin County has been called, by water researchers who know that its municipalities draw on relatively small reservoirs in the hills. There are no mountainous, snow-fed sources nearby. During drought, which is common here, coastal rivers to the north are tapped through an elaborate system of plumbing. Water flows toward money, which Marin has in abundance. Median household income: $104,000.

Yet even among the abundance, one can find monk-like austerity at the meditation center. Tiny rooms. Narrow beds. A single chair and bedside lamp. Miniscule in-room sinks. Sleeping halls that are quiet and warm. Stealthy, radiant heat. Meditation and dining halls open around the clock. It's all more than enough. (As I overhear one yogi say before the week's official silence begins, "Who gets to do this?" as she marvels at the unlimited tea and snacks.) Plenitude indeed, even if reading and writing are not allowed.

I hike bay-scented trails as the day fades. Stands of forest cling to the north slopes. Out among the silent trees, I drink huge draughts of air.

WHAT DREW ME TO THIS CENTER, AFTER DECADES OF LIVING nearby and rarely thinking of venturing here? Fatigue. Despair driven in part by a constant grief about climate and water. An undercurrent of pain runs through many in the community where I lived for years, working in the beleaguered creeks and rivers. Those formerly blue-ribbon steelhead streams are drawn down, largely because of the agricultural and urban growth in Sonoma County. For decades I took part in conversations about which shift in thought or behavior would result in the best and most change.

I'm far from the only one in agony about current trends in water use, drought, climate, and wildlife decline. There are plenty of others feeling the pain. Some are acting; some wondering how to act. To the Buddhist practitioner, knowing what to do and not knowing are held in balance. It's been the way of those who've been sitting for enlightenment for 2,600 years. Much of the teaching is about insight and growth. Much, too, is about acceptance.

There's a yin and yang in tolerance and action. Knowing one's place in the world, both small and great, is an acquired wisdom. As Zen poet Gary Snyder has said, "Knowing that nothing need be done is where we begin to move from."

~

IT'S SOLSTICE WEEK. *SOLSTICE*, WHERE WE'RE INVITED TO DIVE into the fertile darkness of the season. From the Latin *sol* (sun) plus *stit* (stopped), *solstice* means "stationary sun." The sun doesn't halt in its tracks; even I, with a sketchy grasp of astronomy, know that *el sol* continues to rotate despite this name. It moves with gaseous, uneven, ball-of-fire magnificence. Earth likewise continues its rotations, as the northern hemisphere goes through its shortest days and longest nights of the year.

The interminable nights are powerful. Hibernatory. They pull on us to stay in bed until the light returns. The retreat schedule, though, demands otherwise.

Our three instructors arrive to the spacious meditation hall one by one. They each greet a Buddha statue at the front of the room with ritual—bowing, nodding, or clasping hands. We student yogis face forward in silence as the *dharma* talks begin. I listen with eyes closed, eyes open, sometimes aware of others in the hall, sometimes not. From stillness comes insight, we're told. The darkness of solstice is generative, substantive—a time to contemplate creativity. Part of the practice, though, is to refrain from working out life's challenges while we're here. We're just to *be*. If we do the practice, solutions may come, but it's not our end-goal to find answers.

We sit. We chant. We listen. Outside the big windows, the sky grows dim. I wonder what nocturnal animals and birds move around the hall as we sit motionless. I'm used to moving, as they do. I find the stillness challenging.

Two hours of deep silence later, we're dismissed. It's quiet in the foyer, quiet as we patter away on asphalt paths. The night is bracing. The cold Pacific air penetrates my coat like icy water. All around, on the paths back to the residences, there are no words, just the fleeting screech of a barn owl and the whisper of tree boughs. Near my own hall, named *Metta* for loving

79

kindness, I stop to find the Big and Little Dippers and the North Star (Polaris) that binds them. They're over the hills that are called mountains in California. In Sonoma Valley, I'd be seeing them through a familiar break in the neighbors' trees.

TOILET CLEANING GETS A BAD RAP THAT ON MOST DAYS IS well earned. There's the general affront to one's nostrils. The seats and bowls may show the signs of prior users in unpleasant ways. There are persistent stains that challenge the diligent, rubber-gloved semiprofessional like myself, assigned to housekeeping for my "work meditation" (a label that I suspected was euphemistic). I've cleaned toilets forever—port-a-potties as a river guide, outhouses as a river ranger, motel rooms as a temporary ski-town maid, everything as a single mom. Now I tackle the two bathrooms, French doors, and entrance hall for the meditation center's dining room.

Wipe windows, mirrors, fixtures, and door handles with disinfectant. Scrub out sinks and toilet bowls with Bon Ami cleanser. Empty trashcans but leave recycling for a different yogi. Sweep or vacuum floors and welcome mats. Mop. Take used cleaning rags to the laundry room and bring back new ones.

As I work on Day Two, I'm aware of everything and everybody: the staffers who show me where supplies are without breaking silence; the younger yogis who were assigned cushy patio sweeping jobs; the constant coming and going of people through the French doors; the yogis who bow respectfully before stepping inside; the yogis who don't.

After work meditation, I walk up a ravine tucked among straw-colored hills to the west. On top, I veer toward the call of a wren in a cluster of oaks. Canopies of the windswept trees meet like open umbrellas at their rounded edges. The whoosh of the commuter road just off-site persists at the base of these slopes. Somewhere down there, too, is the center's boundary line. Across the valley are the distinct, flat roofs of a wastewater treatment plant. Its buildings are set back from the road, not easily viewed by motorists but obvious to hikers, who have a hawk's-eye perspective of them.

Ponds like these aren't highlighted on tourist's maps. Tanks of offal don't attract the everyday globetrotter, but they have their aficionados in bird lovers, who are attracted to wastewater treatment facilities as if they're gold. *Alluring*, I've heard expert birders call them. *Multi-faceted. Teeming and birdy.* Treatment ponds are a reliable source of open water, nutrients, and plant life for wildlife in general, sometimes their only refuge for miles. Within this geography, the urban-wildland interface, sewage ponds are the only oases around.

My life list of birds, far from exhaustive, is populated with plenty of species seen first at treatment ponds. Hawaiian stilt, bridled titmouse, plumbeous vireo, yellow-headed blackbird, American tree sparrow, gray flycatcher, solitary sandpiper. Some are birds I haven't seen anywhere else. The first and only time I've seen a Harris's sparrow, for instance, was at the Las Gallinas sewage ponds about a half hour's drive from the meditation center. The sparrow scratched the ground with an exuberant push-hop unlike the foraging of the white-crowned sparrows all around it. A dozen pairs of binoculars and scopes were focused on the Harris's when I arrived; it took me thirty seconds to spot it.

The tanks across the road from the meditation center don't receive our five to ten thousand gallons of daily, silently deposited waste. The center has its own sewage-treatment system, considered large capacity. Our offerings are dispersed on-site, that is, into a septic system. It seems to handle everything we can throw at it, although as good retreatants and responsible adults, we're not to feed it anything but waste and toilet paper. Like everything else here, we yogis follow instructions and don't talk about it.

LATER ON DAY TWO, I'M IN PHYSICAL PAIN. MY BACK HURTS. My teeth are on edge. Yesterday I sat with knees crossed for the better part of fourteen hours. Today I'm in my twelfth hour and counting. My head aches—it's throbbing. Maybe because I forgot to drink my habitual black tea after the morning bell? Or is it this interminable *sitting*? I begin judging others with a vengeance. One instructor's eyes are too big and intense. Another instructor points in an imperious manner as she speaks. Our discomfort is about ourselves, she says, but I'm pretty sure it's about her. The third instructor laughs at his own jokes, a nerdy habit that I usually find charming. Today I only find it annoying.

I'm not sure that I'm going to make it. What kind of out do they offer from this place?

Many of the cushions were empty at this morning's 6:15 *qigong* practice and meditation, and many seats are empty now, midday. We're maintaining silence, of course, so I don't ask where anyone has gone and why. It's inappropriate to focus on anything but my breath, anyway. The missing are simply missing.

After dinner the pointing instructor gives a talk about transformation. "What if you knew the person beside you would someday save your life?" she asks, suggesting that the annoying snorer to my left might turn Good Samaritan in my hour of need. I drift in and out of sleep. The instructor may be right, but I don't care. I'm strangely obdurate. This is supposed to be of value, but how? The instructors seem somber. The retreatants are irritating, the meditation hall unsettled with coughing fits and sneezes. I'm supposed to stay within myself while those around me are spreading winter flu bugs through the air? The hours stretch interminably long.

A more experienced practitioner could tell me that I'm suffering Second Day Syndrome. New retreatants often take time to settle into the silence and stillness of meditation. It takes three days to really *be* here. The first two days of a sitting residency, then, are something we must pass through on the way to enlightenment.

Tomorrow is the actual day of winter solstice, *the* day. In those shortest of sunlit hours, I'm required to attend a small group meeting, but I don't want to break the Noble Silence. *Noble*, per the *Oxford English Dictionary*, "having or showing fine personal qualities" and "of excellent or superior quality." Confident that I want to maintain the silence for its excellence, rather than because I'm feeling superior, I write the instructor a note begging off.

On Day Three, I again tackle work meditation and cleaning the porcelain thrones that flush away our waste. My knees are bruised from prior cleanings. My back aches. I dive into the work, anyway, calculating its value. If the average US citizen eliminates a daily amount of solids weighing 128 grams or 4.5 ounces, then the center's approximately one hundred retreatants are dumping over 28 pounds of poop each day. Over six days, therefore, we're mixing 168 pounds of waste with the water that carries it off to the septic system. Then, unlike a wastewater treatment plant, which would actively remove solids and divert water for further treatment, the septic system will settle out solids and release effluent to a drainfield.

Either method of separating liquid from sludge makes possible the return of water to the environment, but only after it's clean enough. Some systems then proceed to use a natural "polishing" procedure that incorporates wetland plants, soils, and their associated microbes to do the ultimate cleaning. Polishing wetlands are the ecosystems birds love.

No two ways about it—in a commons used by one hundred souls, this work detail is needed every single day. The toilets are used pretty hard due to the sheer numbers of yogis walking past this particular spot for snacks and meals. Clearly my work detail is important, I tell myself. My mind dwells on my own significance in the scheme of things. When I catch myself thinking rather than staying in meditative mode, I switch to a technique we've been taught to keep our very human brains from *storytelling*.

Not now, I mind-chant. *Not now*, I tell the storyteller in me. As my active brain wanders through memories and explanations, I repeat: *Not now. Later.*

Earlier this morning, one of the instructors shared a Jane Hirshfield poem. Because we'd been given permission to do so, I jotted one line from the poem in my otherwise neglected journal: *you will recognize what I am saying or you will not.* Hirshfield didn't write this about housekeeping, but it applies. Some people will recognize the transient pain of the window washer. Some will not—and those are the ones who leave big, flowery imprints of their fingers and palms on the glass the moment it's clean and gleaming. Of course they do.

Now, in contemplation, something clicks in me. Cleaning is impermanent, as is everything in life. Work meditation is a lesson in the fleeting quality of life. Why despair at the hard work of it, or judge those who don't recognize that? Somehow this frees me. I finish cleaning the mirrors, windows, sinks, toilets, and floors with lightning speed.

When time comes for the small group meeting, I attend. The heretofore-imperious instructor, who replied to my note from yesterday with an understanding and nonjudgmental response, accepts my arrival with equanimity. She is gentle and joyful and knows just what to say. Emotions among the student yogis are running high, but she has wise advice tailored to everyone, from those who are giddy to those who weep. She tells us to stick with it. Stay here. Just do the practice. Great rewards will come if we sit with this day, this way.

Indoors, I sit and breathe. Outdoors, I engage in walking meditation. Whatever arises, I breathe. At the solstice dusk, which settles with startling haste, a great-horned owl calls from the forest across the creek. I breathe.

SEWAGE TREATMENT DOESN'T ENTER MY MIND DURING DAY Four's work meditation. The breathing practice helps me take a break from my obsession and pain over water. *In-pause-out. In-pause-out.* One instructor has advised us to insert the word *pause* in the space between inhaling and exhaling, because in that instant our minds like to wander. We plot *when-I'm-done-with-this-I'm-gonna . . . and then I'm gonna . . . and then I'm gonna.* Ad infinitum.

In-pause-out. In-pause-out. For all the toilets I've cleaned, I've never tackled them as part of meditative practice. Now I do, and it's revelatory. Work meditation is clearly not just an assignment designed to extract free labor from me. *In-pause-out. In-pause-out.* Without trying, I again finish in a fraction of the time of the first cleanings.

Afterward, I take to the hills. Following a trail through coyote brush, up a gully, past a shrine and sitting bench, I find myself going farther, all the way to the east ridge. Up there the footpath intersects a fire road that goes in both directions, conceivably forever. A staffer is returning along the road from the north, her cheeks flushed with exertion. She keeps a steady pace, the ends of her bobbed hair fringed from a wool cap, her coat tied around her waist. In a quick gesture, she presses her palms together over her heart, acknowledging me without slowing down.

I view the surrounding hills that recede in misty layers with distance. The center and water treatment plant across the road are like tiny villages seen on a map. They're fine and private places. Both are reminders that we all must sit and empty our bowels as well as our minds.

In California, as around the world, water is the medium we use to flush waste. We could substitute the heat of fire or the decaying processes of composting on a large scale. We're not there yet, though. We're still fouling our own drinking water, the very liquid every living thing needs to survive. Stopping that would be a giant step toward preserving the green sanctuaries we have left. Robert Frost wrote, "Some say the world will end in fire / Some say in ice." I say we'll endure or end by the grace of water. Our future rests in part with treatment plants, the best of which serve not only as habitat and refuge for birds and wildlife but also as parks and preserves for human rest, recreation, and recycling the world's most precious compound.

Day Five, our last full day, arrives too fast. At the same time, it's taken forever to get here, with the elastic sense of time inherent in retreat. We go through training in how to break our silence, a bit at a time, like dipping toes into a pool before diving in. We speak to the practitioners who've been sitting to our left and right for the past week, for the first time looking them full in the face and trying out our voices. We're told when to start and when to stop, but when asked to end their stream of words, people keep going. They chatter on like a river flowing. My mind buzzes with my own voice, as if someone has unleashed a hive of bees into my brain. The words, the eye contact, the listening—all are startling following the days of quiet contemplation.

We're also told how to continue our practice back in the real world. We're advised to take the quality of deeper attention into our daily work. Pause in conversation long enough to let the impulses from our brains reach our hearts before we act. Incorporate meditative practice into the flow of our life, as we've done with work meditation while here at the center. In this way our lives become our practice. In this way we can open our hearts. *May all that covers my heart be dissolved.*

When deciding how to treat our beautiful planet, we can use this same pause to show respect for the water we use—our lifeblood. The retreat center's literature asked us to take a mindful pause in noting *the drought may seem over.* The word *seem* provides a cautious, polite, guarded side to any message, allowing a moment between inhalation and exhalation. From the old Norse *sœma*, the little word means "to honor," as in easing the path of communications by giving them time to breathe.

If only our world was just seeming to be in drought. Months after leaving the retreat, I find evidence everywhere that the drought that seemed over in December is nowhere near done. Headlines proclaim: "The 'New Normal'? Sierra Snow Drought Endures Despite 'Miracle' March," "Oregon Governor Declares Drought Emergency in Second County," "Wheat Markets Eye Expanding Drought in US Plains," and "Highest Drought Intensity Returns to Arizona."

We are deep into it. Like the darkness of solstice, increased aridity is real, tangible, and everywhere. Those of us who've experienced a well going dry know that even a seasonal failure is a terrifying thing. In the United States, several years of below-average rainfall have pushed agricultural and urban communities to overdraw groundwater. We also draw more from wild rivers or the aquifers that feed them. Around the world, too, water shortages pose humanitarian crises. In Somalia, for instance, failing water supplies have led to widespread, fatal, waterborne disease; the United Nations has said that *half of that country's population* is in danger of perishing from drought-related famine. In South Africa's worst natural disaster in thirty years, reservoirs stand twenty-six percent full. These are mere examples. According to the *Bulletin of the Atomic Scientists*, Cape Town recently added a new term to the English vocabulary: *Day Zero*, "the day the taps go dry."

We're ready for a sea change, a move to inherent knowing that water is no different from our bodies, ourselves. If our souls are our essence—the essential human self embodied in us—then the fact of our bodies consisting of up to sixty percent water helps define our souls. We can relate to a river not just as an aqueduct for our needs but as a true part of cultural, physical, and spiritual fabric. Our beloved children, too, are precious walking, talking containers of essential fluid that can only be sustained with more of the same. It's on us to give them that.

Indigenous wisdom tells us that every living thing is sacred. So does the Buddhist practice of consuming moderately and allowing all life to thrive. Water can be a great teacher, the Buddha of compounds. As author Barry Lopez wrote in the essay "Drought," in *River Notes*: "I fasted and abstained as much as I felt appropriate from water. These were only gestures, of course, but even as a boy I knew a gesture might mean life or death and I believed the universe was similarly triggered."

Not a popular creed these days, to use mindfully at least in gesture, but that is where meditation takes us. To pause and then to allow. Using only the water that's needed for life embraces both the power of individual gesture and the respect for water in nature to replenish our ecosystems. To the Buddhists, too, modest consumption is part of the path toward enlightenment. The center's gracious words about water use, integrating the word *seem*, weave with its philosophy of walking lightly over the earth.

THE MORNING OF OUR DEPARTURE, I DIVE INTO ONE LAST work meditation. Something about the frequency of my cleaning has made its impermanence more acceptable. The yogis who leave handprints with thoughtless abandon may not see that mindfulness extends to those who serve them, but it's not my job to police that. Nothing lasts, perhaps especially in the world of cleaning, but the glass can be wiped again. When I'm done, the bathrooms and hallway sparkle, ready for the next set of yogis to arrive. I sweep and dust my room. I scrub my own sink, shine my own mirror.

As I wheel my luggage down the hill from Metta, the Noble Silence has lifted all around me. The air fills with words and a sense of elation. Faces glow. Voices carry a lightness. I neither rush to speak nor hurry to read or write or turn on my cell phone. The joy of this passing moment fills my heart. I swallow the woodsy air. Statues of the Buddha remain in their serene vigils by the paths.

A hand-lettered sign is the last thing I see as I depart: *May All Beings Be Stoked.* Great adjective, *stoked*, meaning "euphoric" or "excited." Then there's the verb, *to stoke*, "to fire up," "to feed." Leaving the center, I'm all of the above—fortified, fueled, thrilled, high—but with an electricity that's grounded. From this energized place, I cross the center boundary. From this knowing that nothing need be done, I begin to move.

7.

The Lone Kayaker

D USK ON THE RIVER. MY FELLOW NATIONAL PARK SERVICE
river ranger Fred Bunch and I had taken turns digging
an outhouse pit through river sand and gravel. He'd almost
finished the last shoveling and was standing in an excavation
that extended over his head. It was time for him to either quit
or stay down there forever. I gave him a hand out. He lay down
his shovel and shook the dust off his NPS ballcap. As we stood
up the bank from shore, dirty and exhausted, we glimpsed the
unexpected: a solo kayaker paddling the rapids that ran past
our camp. Tired to the point of giddiness, Fred and I laughed.
We didn't trust our eyes. The boater had to be a mirage, rising
and falling over waves that reflected back a golden sunset.

We'd brought a law enforcement ranger on our trip that
week, though, and he wasn't under the same delusion that
gripped Fred and me. He hadn't been digging and so had gotten a better look at the kayaker. Without a word to us, he pulled
out his two-way radio to call a backcountry station forty-five
miles downstream.

"Lone kayaker passing Anderson Hole at 1930 hours," the
ranger-cop said. "He's headed your way."

Fred and I met eyes. We'd grasped the situation an instant
after the ranger-cop had. Any permitted boaters would've
launched hours before and already passed the beach where

we'd stopped for camping and digging. The kayaker must've put on the water without a permit—breaking a cardinal rule of boating in the national monument. He'd probably happened on our raft patrol by chance and simply kept going in hopes we wouldn't give chase.

He had to know that he was breaking the rules. They were posted everywhere at park headquarters, at the boat ramp, and in NPS brochures (this was at least two decades before websites became primary sources of information for parks and preserves). He had to know that the NPS wouldn't have allowed his trip. Still, the river and its wild canyon, vast silences, soothing calm reaches, and sparkling rapids must've called to him with siren insistence. Given that allure, he'd opted not to hang around in a small town in rural Utah or Colorado, where boaters for that river spent their off-days waiting for the next put-in.

The lone kayaker had answered the call to the oasis in deliberate defiance of the rules. He'd put on the water anyway.

LAST SPRING, I VISITED HUDEMAN SLOUGH IN THE NAPA-Sonoma marshes. I'd gotten up before dawn to explore the wetlands for signs of ducks, owls, sparrows, and geese. From the levees, on which walkways are managed for pedestrian use by the US Fish and Wildlife Service, I'd seen everything I'd hoped for except the great horned owl that often hunts there. Breeding season was in full swing. Little flocks of gadwalls and Canada geese swam the ponded areas, which were rich with red-winged blackbirds, Savannah sparrows, song sparrows, and marsh wrens in surrounding cattails and coyote brush. All was well until a couple of black-necked stilts, long-legged shore-birds that spend their days bobbing their heads and hunting for food, took to shrieking and flapping wings and making short, intense, hopping flights. Something posed a threat. They had to be nesting to be exerting themselves like warriors. They had to have eggs.

Immediately I guessed that a predator had moved close. I set up my birding scope beside the low-lying wetlands to see what was up. I peered into the marshy area from the wide trail on one of the levees that keep brackish tidal water from surrounding alfalfa fields.

In an instant, an unleashed black Labrador retriever ran into my scope view, a playful, half-grown dog frolicking toward the stilts. He galloped toward the panicking birds and plunged through soft herbaceous growth along the water. He might've been finding eggs. I don't know. I do know that, unknown to him, he'd just violated a refuge in which black-and-white winged parents are protected so they can birth and raise their young. Despite the frequent and clear postings that it's a wildlife refuge and no dogs are allowed, much less off leash, here he was.

I leaned back from the spotting scope. The dog's owners strolled past me, deep in conversation and not seeing the drama. They looked at peace, perhaps happy to be outdoors with their manic dog leaving them alone for a few minutes. They appeared to be completely oblivious to the life-and-death crisis they'd created. They glanced at my scope and binoculars and smiled.

"Have you seen lots of good birds?" they asked.

WILDLIFE PRESERVES AND REFUGES HAVE DIFFERENT RULES than dog parks, urban playgrounds, and rural ranches. In my experience as a guide and ranger, as well as a recreational boater, hiker, skier, and cyclist, I've run across plenty of users in the act of defying the rules. Puzzling over this, I quizzed several dozen friends of all backgrounds on why they break the rules outdoors. One-third said that they never had. The other two-thirds admitted to going beyond a marked boundary, entering a protected area without a permit, walking a leashed or unleashed pet in a restricted area, and doing other forbidden things despite postings. Some said they'd gone further than any of the above, by ignoring mandatory safety regulations or going into a natural area closed to all entry.

If I'd taken the survey myself, I'd have listed some of these same infractions. Most of the lines I'd crossed were many years behind me, before I worked for agencies charged with protecting the land. That is, the field crews spent their days policing and enforcing while the higher-ups made deals and rules. To be fair, many found themselves in positions that had long since catered to corporate interests and consumer demand. National forests were harvested and scalped. National monuments lay open to off-road use that threatened wildlife species and native habitat. Set beside that, the crossing by boundaries on foot or by boat seemed a small thing. Many see it as their birthright—I surely had.

Then I came to understand that these parks and preserves were islands of natural habitat in our stressed world. Like oases, they are gems in a tarnished crown. We may have limited control over what goes on with government—although we can vote, register comments, support representatives who are really representative, and protest corruption—but we do control the smaller, human-sized actions that affect wildlife and habitat.

Our individual actions may have bigger consequences than we know. Research shows, for instance, that the mere presence of domestic dogs outdoors drives wildlife from protected areas. Like the black-necked stilts at Hudeman, the refugees have to take their chances in less friendly habitat. A Colorado State University study showed significantly fewer mule deer, small mammals, prairie dogs, and bobcats in preserves where dogs were allowed. Similarly, dogs who flush or chase triggers avian flight distance—the number of feet or yards at which birds flee from perceived danger. They lose time and energy for feeding, resting, or tending young. It's stressful. It's like a stranger plunging into the middle of a family home, knocking over a beloved toddler's highchair, and trampling its meal underfoot.

When it comes to stress, it's about the hormones. A wild animal's version of cortisol kicks in when we bring four-legged, domestic predators into their habitat. It doesn't matter to the wildlife whether an area is posted or not. Stress-level monitoring of Swiss Alps grouse at the urban-wild interface—that is, near recreational or population centers—shows that birds go into crisis response when they come upon perceived predators. Dogs on and off trails matter. Hikers do, too. That small bit of sanctuary critical to the wild bird is violated as surely as if it were a hydric zone drawn down by pumping.

Research on humans venturing outdoors points to a range of reasons why we break rules. Whether we're aware of it or not, we may be going for a cheater's high. Psychologists say that good moods follow on the heels of getting away with a transgression—beating the odds, say—even if we feel remorse later. Or we believe that our infractions won't hurt anyone. Most of the outdoor rule breakers I quizzed said they'd chosen to break rules that made no sense to them, or because others had broken them before, or because they believed that the consequences of their actions wouldn't be significant. Without examining the data, they'd ignored the postings of those who called the shots and made their own choices.

So human.

"MOST PEOPLE DON'T HAVE A FULL UNDERSTANDING OF THE fragility of the system or wildlife in it," says former state park ecologist and national park backcountry ranger Jeannine Koshear. "Rangers and park managers are tasked with protecting both. You can't do that unless you limit visitation. Take the rules about bears in Sequoia National Park. The rules protect the bears from people and the people from the bears. The rules are there because people have a history of past abuses in approaching wildlife or sensitive areas. The rules are not just for the sake of making rules."

Places like Sequoia provide havens for visitors. Likewise, these green refuges of diverse habitat provide safe space for wild flora and fauna. Outside park boundaries, protected wildlife become targets for those who don't believe in the wisdom of endangered-species legislation or managed lands. Regulations are often put in place after much deliberation, review of data, and public vetting. Many boundary crossers do little to no research but perceive postings as arbitrary and limiting and just plain nonsense. We venture outdoors with our own sort of flight distance, the need for space from rules and other visitors. Many of us want to be free of management control, so going beyond a boundary becomes part of the experience: "Going somewhere alone was the goal—to go off trail, into a closed locale" or "I didn't go into the wilderness to stay on a marked trail" or "I hate cairns, so I knocked them all down."

And there's the rub. Rangers like Fred and me were hired to help protect the wilderness experience on a remote river. Those who'd waited their turn and adhered to the rules of the game expected to be rewarded with a pristine environment. To get out there and find pirate trails, non-permitted boaters, and rogue campers (private boaters in Grand Canyon are notorious for overstaying on beaches in defiance of regulations) sullies the wilderness experience for those who've played it square. "If I can't break the rules, neither can you," one survey respondent wrote.

The danger that Jeannine mentioned is very real. In snow sports, for one, boundary crossers pose risk to other people, infrastructure, and the environment. The Utah Avalanche Center notes that most avalanche fatalities are triggered by people unaware of the hazards involved in skiing or boarding out of bounds. The center advises, "You can't go straight from being a resort skier to having all the knowledge and wisdom for safe backcountry travel." Among its many examples of skier- and boarder-triggered incidents involving noncompliance, the center cites a recent hundred-year avalanche near Jackson

Hole, Wyoming, that buried a creek drainage twenty to thirty feet deep in debris. The cause? An out-of-bounds recreationist. Out of sheer luck, no people were hurt downslope from the freedom-seeker.

RECENTLY I BIRDED AMONG HILLY PUBLIC LANDS IN NORTHERN California with my brother and his wife. The morning had broken quiet and cool. Small clouds drifted overhead. We spotted plenty of hawks, waterfowl, woodpeckers, and songbirds from trails that led to one of the area's only small reservoirs on state-owned property. The "lake" pipes directly to a water treatment system that's used for a center for developmentally disabled adults. Geese and ducks nest alongshore. Songbirds live and breed in thick vegetation directly on the water. Dog walkers gravitate to the lake, too, happily, blithely. Despite postings about the risk of *E. coli* contamination inherent in canine trespass into the drinking water, dog owners encourage their pets to take the plunge—sometimes as they watch over their shoulders, looking to see if any enforcers are around.

We strolled toward the water. A woman passed us, her German shepherd running off leash and thrashing through scrub where we'd just heard the rustle of lizards or snakes.

My very polite sister-in-law pointed to a *Dogs Must Be on Leash* sign. "You know," she said, in a sweet voice, "that says that your dog should be on leash."

The woman didn't look up. She didn't reply—she barked. If we hadn't seen her lips move, we wouldn't have known whether we'd heard her sharp voice or her shepherd's. My brother and I stared at each other with big eyes as if we'd fallen down some rabbit hole. The woman and her dog headed straight for the lake, scattering nesting red-winged blackbirds.

IF WE KNOW THAT BREAKING RULES TRAMPLES THE SMALL percentage of natural lands set aside for wildlife and water purity, are we deterred? Not really, according to recreation research. Instead it shows a direct correlation between compliance and consequences only when the latter are seen as significant. An Ohio State University study of behavioral norms in the wild concluded that the more certain the rule and the sanctions for breaking it, the more likely it is to be followed. Protecting habitat or even our own drinking water doesn't sway most of us. Wishing not to get search-and-rescue teams out of their warm beds at night for no good reason doesn't, either. The firm consequence of a five-thousand-dollar fine, however, might. That's what the lone kayaker would risk today, as well as banishment from the river for a year, were he caught paddling without a permit.

Climate change, deforestation, rampant land acquisition for oil development—all beat wilderness infractions hands down with regard to impact. It's not the dogs that are driving the world to the dogs, say the dog lovers. Who can fault the owners who just want to get their best friends out on the trail and into the joys of nature? Nobody, perhaps, except the park ranger who pointed it out to me—that urban-interface wild areas are home to wildlife populations that remain vulnerable to our use. He was one of the educated and experienced resource managers who we pay to protect these lands.

We commend our public trust to these managers in dollars and pledges. And then we run over their efforts to protect wild lives, even at the water's edge, the very oases in our midst.

On that river years ago, Fred and I didn't apprehend the lone kayaker. Had we immediately dropped our shovels and followed him in our rafts, we'd never have caught him in his sleeker craft. He knew it, but having seen us must have given him a scare. He paddled past the downstream ranger stations by night. He hid and slept by day. Weeks afterward, when I met him at a dinner party, one of my friends confided his identity to me. I shook the kayaker's hand and didn't let on what I knew.

He didn't either. Fred and I did spend the rest of the summer watching more carefully, having conversations that helped make our presence known while accepting the limitations to our really protecting the river.

The lone kayaker told me some time later that he'd suffered no consequences. He considered the impact of his trip insignificant.

He'd lost our trust, of course, something in the fellowship of river runners that was rarely breached. The river was sacred space, the holy divinity of water. Years later I heard that he'd also breached agreement on a Colorado River trip that had run low of rations; he snuck in for more than his share. Maybe once a rule breaker, always a rule breaker. A later infraction on a different continent would cost him a job, levy a fine, result in deportation, and eliminate several prospects he'd had for future employment. Those consequences, he confided to a mutual friend, were significant.

8.

FIRST RESPONDERS

S UNDAY EVENING, OCTOBER 8, 2017. PAUL AND I ARE SIT-
ting with friends after dinner, lingering late in our dining
room in Sonoma, when a jolt of wind hits the house. Our open
windows shake with the force. Gusts reach gale intensity all at
once, leashed things now let loose. Leaves and branches batter
the glass, debris tossed from live oaks on the hill behind us and
Douglas firs toward the street. The tops of redwoods bend and
pitch. We who are sitting at the table meet cautious eyes. We've
been living with an unprecedented dryness in Sonoma Valley,
the forests thick with parched ground cover. Biologists have
called our premature fall of leaves "leaf drop," a sign of plants
unhappy with their environment. El Niño conditions of last
winter, with double the average precipitation for our region,
were followed by the hottest summer on record. Woods are
thick with understory that subsequently desiccated, creating
standing tinder around the thousands of homes on the many
streets that wind through the numerous hills and fields of our
hometown. Everything is ready to burn.

We do—and don't—recognize this wind. "Fire wind," I say,
although I've never known it to go from zero to sixty in an
instant. In Southern California, the Santa Anas whip off nearby
deserts and down canyons toward the coastal plain, sucked
toward lower pressures at the ocean. Threat of fire rides the winds

into neighborhoods and towns. In Northern California, the process is the same, but we call the winds *Diablo*. Devil winds. What we don't know yet is that meteorologists will label this a two-hundred-year weather event. Days later we'll hear radio broadcasters describe these winds as the strongest Diablos in our lifetimes, with an unprecedented pressure differential between the highs inland and the lows over the ocean. Hearing their analysis, I'll instantly recall the many years of rain events that I monitored in Sonoma as a stream researcher. They once came in predictable patterns, so much so that we who managed restoration projects knew when to expect wet season to begin, stopping all construction. Now such predictability is out the window. Rainfall so intense that it occurs only every hundred years comes whenever it wants. Streams flood more frequently than in the past. The Diablos of today aren't likely to follow old patterns, either. I'd bet all my nickels that we'll see many more two-hundred-year events in our lifetimes, blowing the roof off current weather reporting.

Stepping out to the front porch, we discover that the wind is cool, unlike the Santa Anas. Leaves and twigs swirl in chaotic vortices. We part for the night. Paul and I don't know that we won't see our friends again until weeks after entire neighborhoods have burned and ours has evacuated wholesale.

THAT NIGHT, WE CLOSE OUR WINDOWS. WE ALMOST NEVER sleep with them closed in late summer and fall, but if they're open on a night like this, we'll only be kept awake. Every creak and groan will sound like falling trees. Huge oaks and firs have moaned and crashed to earth more than once here, in much lesser winds. They've blocked our passage for days as we've worked to clear the way. So far, nothing big has collapsed on the house, but they've come close. The falling limbs of bay and oak have swished their leaves and smaller branches against our walls on their way down.

I sleep until six a.m.—late for me. Our power is off, with no whir of clocks or refrigerator. That's unusual; I step outside to ask if the neighbors have electricity and to see how our trees fared in the night. The winds have calmed, but the sky is dust-brown to the west and south. Black-edged plumes rise to the east. Smoke. Ash falls everywhere, small white flakes like snowfall, but dry, as on extremely cold ski days. The morning is quiet, eerily so. There aren't even the oddly reassuring sounds of firefighters' sirens or rumble of planes that usually accompany smoke. The smell of the morning is sour, not the scent of clean coals burning but more like smoldering trash. Something is burning somewhere or, by the looks of things, everywhere.

The first text comes from my daughter in Seattle. "Are you guys OK?" The national news says Sonoma County is burning up, she writes. Several neighborhoods to the north were either razed by fire or evacuated in the night.

She urges us to get updates by texting our zip code to 888777. We do and see that California Department of Forestry and Fire Protection (CAL FIRE) evacuations are proceeding north to south in neighborhood-sized blocks, ahead of a "fire complex" that's marching down Sonoma Valley and coming our way. Like the fire drills we used to do in grade school, where the classrooms emptied out one at a time, we're to exit the valley when we're told.

Along with having no power, we have no internet. Our cell phones are working but with little reception in our wooded canyon, so every message we send is by text. We do the old-fashioned thing and walk up our wooded driveway to talk to neighbors. They're standing in the middle of the street, arms folded over their chests, sharing what they've learned. They've gotten news by cell phone or by talking to someone who's talked to someone else who knows an emergency worker or a friend who's already been evacuated. A dog nobody knows is wandering from driveway to driveway. An entire heritage oak has collapsed onto a neighbor's lawn (the only lawn on our street kept green through the drought). We swap emergency gear: windup radios, spare breathing masks, gasoline in five-gallon containers.

Entire neighborhoods are gone in Santa Rosa. Fires have sprung up all over the North Bay, and no firefighters are here because they're all busy with evacuations. If the winds come up again, our neighborhood will be next.

The verdant town of Glen Ellen, five miles north, has burned down. Or so we hear. My friend Arthur Dawson lives there. Later he'll tell me that he and his wife, Jill, evacuated at two a.m., just ahead of a voracious, flaming monster called the Nuns Fire. They were woken by emergency workers who ordered them to get out in fifteen minutes. With son Larkin, family dog Pepper, and two cats Peeka and Boo, Jill and Arthur fled to a friend's home on Madrone Road. At nine a.m., Madrone had evacuation orders, too, and the Dawsons found refuge farther south with other friends in Boyes Hot Springs. Days later, when Boyes was under evacuation advisory and the air had become unfit to breathe, the Dawsons headed for another friend's place in Marin County.

The Dawsons weren't allowed to go home; in fact they heard via the news that their house had "burned to the ground" that first night, like most of their neighborhood. When the Dawsons fled a third time, and left Sonoma Valley altogether, they crept out in a long line of traffic. A camouflaged National Guard Humvee with a gun turret passed them on the way in.

"Holy shit!" Arthur emailed me, after reaching Nicasio, closer to the coast. "This is the apocalypse."

Days before the fire, I spoke at a Women Writing Science community event with Lisa Micheli, President and CEO of Pepperwood Preserve outside Santa Rosa. We led a discussion on water and science in writing. Water is what brought Lisa and me together in the early 2000s, when we were monitoring Sonoma Valley streams for factors limiting the survival of endangered steelhead trout. The US Environmental Protection Agency funded the work through state and regional outlets. Our results showed that the decline of dry-season stream flows was the biggest threat of many to the survival of oversummering juvenile steelhead. The formerly blue-ribbon trout streams of Sonoma had been drawn down by the water demands of a growing population and a changing agricultural picture from mixed and dry farming to wine grapes. Over the summer seasons, the young fish now perish before they can get to sea.

When asked what we should do about conserving water, Lisa and I both pointed to the self-identified driest continent, Australia. The Aussie solution for storing water Down Under has long been to catch rainfall in decentralized, small holding tanks, beneath or beside every house. California, with its large dams that destroy shady river corridors and species diversity, can learn about climate resilience from those who've lived with extended drought and megafire for longer than we have. Downsizing our water needs leaves more for the green refuges in our world, which—no surprise—reduces the risk of the gigantic fires that threaten everyone.

In his farewell speech, President Obama attempted to internationalize climate action. If we don't act, he said, our children will spend all their time responding to climate change. That reality is already here—any firefighter or wildfire monitor or meteorologist will tell us. It's absolutely time to roll up our sleeves again and say, "We can do it!"

When the Sunday winds kicked up, Pepperwood Preserve was among the first land bases to burn. The fire hit hard and moved fast. Michael Gillogly, Preserve Manager, received a warning call from a neighbor, looked outside, and saw a big orange glow in the sky. He drove down Franz Valley Road, where a wall of fire was coming from the east. He and another driver proceeded back up the road, honking their horns and alerting the neighbors. "If we didn't see lights turn on or anyone come out, we went up to the door," Michael says.

Back at the preserve, he and his wife Ginger and son Loren prepared to leave the home they'd lived in for seventeen years. They found it hard to focus on what to bring as the flames were getting closer. Not wanting to wait too long, Ginger and Loren drove the family cars out Pepperwood's front entrance, but Michael stayed back to move a few preserve vehicles to safer locations. He phoned other people he knew who were in the path of the fire. And, as he fought spot fires around his home with an extinguisher, he watched Pepperwood burn.

"It was just fascinating. The flames didn't all move at the same rate. They'd make quick runs down the ridge-lines, then take a slower time to burn down the side of the ridge. It was a spectacle, just awesome." Michael's tone conveys both wonder and dismay. If it weren't for the fact that homes and lives were being lost that night, he tells me, he'd have found it easier to appreciate that the fire was "pretty amazing."

When the big hill near him went up in a roaring wall of flame that reached the treetops, Michael knew it was time to leave.

He didn't get far along Mark West Springs Road before he saw CAL FIRE trucks parked on the road. None of the firefighters were outside, because the conditions were so bad. He started to pull past them, until a voice over a loudspeaker told him to stop. It said, "You in the white truck, you cannot go forward. You will not survive if you go forward."

That's when things got trickiest. Michael turned around to drive the other way, although he knew that the fire was burning in that direction, too. At Mark West Lodge, he asked another CAL FIRE employee what to do. "I don't know," the employee said. "There are no good options at this point." Michael could stay in a wide part of the road and let the fire burn past and hopefully around him, or he could try to drive out to Calistoga Road.

Michael, along with two other drivers who were also surrounded by fire, decided to make a run through a flaming forest that had been building up understory for years. "For the entire three miles to Calistoga Road, everything was on fire on both sides of us. All the houses, everything we passed, it was all burning. I could feel the heat from inside my cab." Trees had fallen across the way, and rocks dislodged by flames had rolled down a steep bank onto the road. He steered around all of those. "My adrenaline was pumping as I dodged everything, and I had to keep my eyes on the road and go fast, but not so fast that I crashed and lost the opportunity to get out." Soon he was through it, but there would be more driving through hell that night.

He rejoined his family in Santa Rosa and fled south on Highway 101. The fire had reached the freeway from the hills and was jumping over it. People had to get off by driving down on-ramps the wrong way. The wind was blasting, burning embers were flying across the road, and the grass on the shoulders was bursting into flames. "It was just insane," Michael says.

Michael and his family did get out of the fire zone, but they lost their home that night. The preserve where they'd lived for years—that refuge, that sanctuary—went up in flames with everything else. "We always thought that material things weren't that important," Michael says. "Now I see what it means to really lose everything."

TWENTY MILES IN A STRAIGHT LINE FROM THE WORST OF the Tubbs Fire that blackened Pepperwood, the Nuns Fire that took out Glen Ellen is advancing to within five miles of our neighborhood. Rumor has it that entire blocks are being evacuated just one mile away. Paul and I prepare to leave at a moment's notice. We grab food, our earthquake emergency kit, family photos, legal documents, musical instruments, and a few other irreplaceable possessions. We spend the next few hours clearing windfall debris and listening to evacuation alerts on our windup radio. All the information anyone in the neighborhood can get has come by text and over manual and battery-powered radios.

Later, after we leave, we'll have links to maps and broadcasts. We'll have more information than we can imagine. We'll learn that the fire nearest us originated in heavily forested Nuns Canyon, just up now-closed Highway 12. We won't know it until after evacuation, but the Nuns Fire has already joined forces to create fire complexes (or "fire monsters," as we call them) in three directions: the Tubbs Fire that originated near Mount Saint Helena and roared into Pepperwood and Santa Rosa has joined forces with the Pocket, Oakmont, and Nuns Fires to forge the one-hundred-thousand-acre Central Sonoma-Lake-Napa Unit (LNU) Fire Complex. In Napa, just over the Mayacamas Mountains, a similar coalescing of fires is building into the Southern LNU Complex. By tomorrow that will be advancing toward downtown Sonoma.

In the afternoon, I finish packing my car with belongings and drive it up to the street. A sheriff's SUV rolls to a stop at my car. In it are two deputies who've come from Alameda County, part of an inter-agency fire and law-enforcement team that kicks into action for emergencies. One of the two men— both are young enough to be my sons—opens his window. He meets my eyes cautiously, as if he expects me to shout or cry. Instead I ask how things are going. He just nods.

"Is it time to leave?" I ask.

They say yes, the evacuation is voluntary but will soon become mandatory. The deputy nearest me says, "I'd get out if I were you." He rolls up his window. They drive on.

Paul and I convoy out the only road that's still open going

out of town. It's straw-sized and two-lane. The road north is closed due to fire, the road east is barricaded, and the roads south and west have become "parking lots." People haven't been able to get to jobs in adjacent towns or the Bay Area with the roads clogged with evacuees. As we drive out, though, there's a window in traffic. We exit, unobstructed.

FIRE IS A WAY OF LIFE IN CALIFORNIA. AS DEVASTATING A DISaster as this will prove to be, I'm not surprised to see it. All over the West, for more than a decade, scientists have said that wildfires would intensify in number and size. A spray-painted sign in Sonoma Valley puts it more bluntly: "If you can't live like this, you better leave now." It's a sentiment much less endearing than "Stay strong, Sonoma," and "The love in the air is thicker than the smoke," and "Thank you, first responders," which are also spray-painted on plywood signs around town.

Paul and I evacuate toward the coast. We drive through stretches of roadway that are in places more crowded than usual and in others strangely empty. A huge moving van sits at an awkward angle by the side of the road, as if abandoned in a hurry, near a field of grapevines outside Petaluma. A fully loaded station wagon has rolled over in a ditch near the farming community of Two Rock and is being attended by three emergency vehicles. We round a corner and pull to the nonexistent shoulder as a fire engine roars out of the tiny forest town of Occidental. On radio talk shows, people weep over lost homes, the shock of firestorm, and their vanished feeling of security. "Sonoma County is the only place in the world I've ever felt safe," one woman says as she breaks into tears.

I'd expected a natural disaster requiring mass evacuations in the North Bay for many years. As a geologist, I'd pictured something relating to the San Andreas family of faults, predicted to rupture and cause devastation north of San Francisco Bay. Probably, as in 1906, fires would ensue. That so many fires could break out here now, all at once and without earthquake, hadn't occurred to me. We hear over the radio that downed power lines in gale-force winds caused this disaster.

Clearly the first responders knew it could happen. Lives were saved on the first night of the firestorm only because of the heroism and quick response of professionals and volunteers who'd trained to evacuate a dense population. Although responders have been overwhelmed by the size of this blaze, and have called it unimaginable, they're helping the community escape in a preemptive fashion. That, and neighbors have worked together—a grassroots effort using cell phones and word of mouth—to stay current and find housing for evacuees and bring bedding to shelters.

Paul and I continue through the seaside town of Bodega Bay, the scene of another natural disaster, as filmed by Alfred Hitchcock in *The Birds*. Rather than being overrun by crow-like avian aggressors, today Bodega Bay is packed with refugees. The regional park campground at Doran Beach has opened its gates to RVs and tent campers. The roads and sites are more overflowing than on holiday weekends. In Bodega Bay itself, the Grange Hall is mobbed with people both donating supplies and lining up to receive them. Pickup trucks stacked with bottled water, toilet paper, and canned food line the streets. On the radio we hear that Good Samaritans who want to drop off donations should proceed to the Grange.

The clean ocean air of Bodega Bay, far from the nearest fire, offers a break from what people are calling the "Beijing skies" of Sonoma. The index for extremely small particulate matter, or $PM_{2.5}$, in Beijing on Monday was 25. $PM_{2.5}$ at elevated levels irritates our eyes, noses, and respiratory systems; $PM_{2.5}$ counts over 150 aggravate heart and lung disease for anyone. In Sonoma Valley when we left, the count was 403.

We take refuge with retired forester Dave Boyd and ecologist Marla Hastings, both former employees of California

State Parks. They're fire experts, having at times overseen small burns of overgrown forest in the Native American tradition. Dave says that dry winds always come in October, the height of fire season, the last arid days before the rains. The heat in recent seasons is unprecedented, he agrees; things are definitely warmer. He and Marla feel the threat in their home beside a redwood forest that's on their own acreage. They tend it in the way they used to steward the parks, but because the area's small, they thin dead wood in place of burning. Marla says she'd like to "cut a firebreak onto the hill above our house" and save it. She means going in with a bulldozer; she knows exactly how to do it. I wish she could, too, as the inter-agency firefighters and law-enforcement officers aren't around. They're elsewhere fighting the hottest fires. CAL FIRE has thrown five hundred fire engines, thirty-nine helicopters, ten air tankers, ninety-four bulldozers, about five thousand personnel, and nearly one hundred hand crews at the Central LNU Complex alone. The places yet to burn, like our hood, are only on some dim part of anyone's radar.

Marla keeps their car parked nose-out, in good old ranger fashion, ready to roll toward the coast if fires break out in Occidental, too. "It's all downhill to the water from here," she says. Water, where fire stops.

The last thing Paul and I do every night of our weeklong evacuation is check interagency maps for new satellite fire detections in Sonoma Valley. It's the quickest way to get the most targeted information we can find. The red squares and dots that signify new fires as seen from the air are still marching south toward our door and toward the main part of town even farther south. As we research, my gut feels the way it used to when scouting big whitewater in the Grand Canyon: roiling and upset. The dread that our neighborhood could be taken out in minutes is hard to describe any other way; it is a simultaneous gearing up for what might happen and a letting go of controlling the outcome. The house we built fifteen years ago might be spared. It might also turn to rubble overnight.

PEPPERWOOD SYSTEMS ECOLOGIST CELESTE DODGE WAS also watching the fire maps. The sky was falling near her west Sonoma County home—or so it seemed. "Ash rained down for days," she says. She recognized shapes in the descending flakes, those of curtains and house siding and leaves from trees. Clearly she was seeing the ash from burning forests as well as from people's homes. "The most astonishing thing was an old photo, from the 1950s or so, of a mother and a baby. It was barely singed at the edges. I just couldn't believe that it could shoot up into the sky and fly maybe seven miles to land on the sidewalk over here."

Celeste is a fire tracker, someone who grew up in the Sierra Nevada foothills where fire is a way of life. "I'm also a map nerd," she says. The early morning of October 9, she quickly logged onto Google Earth to look at the latest satellite detections for fire. When data goes to Google Earth, it's color-coded for time. New flame detections go from red to orange to yellow every six hours. "The morning of the fire," she says, "every single patch was still red." The fire had burned twelve miles in four hours, from essentially Calistoga to west of Highway 101 in Santa Rosa. In all her years of watching fires, she'd never seen one move so fast.

Celeste would observe some of those red patches firsthand when she made a quick visit to Pepperwood to assess the damage days later. She drove in from the north before the main road reopened, via a back way through an adjoining property. The initial firestorm that destroyed seven thousand or so structures ripped through a neighborhood called Mark West and the southern tip of the preserve. The rest of Pepperwood, from what she could see on the land and by satellite, burned less catastrophically three days later. "So when I first came back, it looked good in terms of what the fire had done to the forest, completely beneficial."

The value of Pepperwood's 3,200 acres became extremely evident during the Sonoma firestorms. Not just living laboratories, where scientists collect data on climate, water, and wildlife, preserves like Pepperwood are land bases on which managers have done controlled burns and firefighters can set breaks to help slow wildfire. "A neighborhood full of houses contains far more fuel per square foot and burns faster," Lisa says. "Nearly all the fire containment done by emergency responders during the Tubbs and Nuns Fires took place in the county's open spaces."

ANOTHER HOME I HELP EVACUATE DURING THE SONOMA FIRES is that of my ninety-four-year-old father and stepmother. On Thursday we see that it's threatened by both the Central LNU Complex and by the Southern LNU Complex in adjacent Napa. Days before, I'd asked our team of caregivers to have the folks ready to drive out of the valley; a ninety-one-year-old relative in the East Bay has offered to take them in. When I call the Dad and Marge on Thursday, mandatory evacuation has extended to within a block of their house. The caregiver agrees that it's time to leave. She mobilizes the folks calmly and quickly, or as quickly as anyone could move two Alzheimer's patients, one with a walker and one so frail she's like a wisp that might blow away. The single road out of town is jammed with evacuees again, but the caregiver gets out without incident. Later I'll hear the stories of other nonagenarian evacuations, some done as group efforts on buses, some done like ours with personal vehicles and individual escape plans.

On Friday I venture back into Sonoma to pick up the personal care items that Dad and Marge have left behind in their haste. The valley air is thick and brown. The Mayacamas Mountains to the east are veiled by smoke, so I can't see the fire shown on the online incident maps. Despite the warnings that say masks can't help with $PM_{2.5}$, I wear one while driving and when I arrive at the house. Ash is falling in Dad and Marge's neighborhood, not just small white flakes but big, poker-chip, carbon-black pieces. Indoors, though, everything is cool and still. The power is on—the home is on a grid that never goes down, as it's close to the hospital and city offices, as well as the high school that's serving as a fire evacuation center.

I pack up Depends, clothes, bathroom items, favorite bed-side books. I pull family photos off the wall and box them in two big cardboard boxes. I stay less than fifteen minutes.

As I drive away, I negotiate a route through the few open streets. Up a side street, a Lexus SUV hesitates at one of countless barricades but then slips around it; I've heard that's been happening all over the county. The asphalt is coated with ash that flies up from my car wheels. Four blocks east I pass an unmarked yellow water truck parked at the corner of MacArthur and Seventh Street East. Two men with full beards and bandanna headscarves, dressed in leathers as if their Other Car Is a Harley, have just loosened the valve on a gray fire hydrant. They grin at each other as the water flows to their truck.

TWO DAYS AFTER EVACUATING PEPPERWOOD, MICHAEL Gillogly returned. He and Lisa drove in with a sheriff escort when it was still an active fire area. He found the sights overwhelming. Throughout the nearby neighborhoods and up Mark West Road, there was hardly a house standing. As far as he could see, homes had been leveled.

The firestorm burned mostly at the southern end of the preserve. After the initial windstorm, there'd been a much less intense burn, a ground fire that traveled slow and low. "You could step over the fire line in places. It kept going and cleaned up the understory. Seeing that, I realized that things were going to be okay. Lots of trees survived. It's not just this burned-over black place, there's still a lot of life." A doe and two fawns who'd frequented the grasslands near Michael's house were still there. In the weeks following the fire, he saw snakes, quail, more deer, a coyote, and other wildlife.

With crisis comes opportunity. Pepperwood's staff got to work immediately, making the best of things. Celeste repaired monitoring equipment as fast as she could. She wanted to study post-fire risks such as debris flow—loose material that moves down mountainsides and hill slopes—and high loads of sediment in our streams. The preserve was the place to do it. She focused first on the core weather stations, in places where she had access. Later, after crews made greater progress clearing wooded areas of dead, standing timber, she reached more remote spots.

Among her other investigations, she wanted to solve a different mystery—one involving the photograph that fell from the sky. "I'd like to return it to the people it belongs to, if I can find them. I'm saving it until I do. It's pretty wild. It's very sad but beautiful at the same time."

Of the Pepperwood staff, Preserve Ecologist Michelle Halbur went through the most devastating loss. Her husband's eighty-year-old parents perished in their home near Cardinal Newman High School. "The sheriff stopped Dave when he went to find them," Michelle said, "so Dave asked him to check on his parents. And the sheriff did go find their bodies."

Remembering her family's huge losses, she also recalled how fortunate she felt to have seen her folks the night before the fires. "Looking back, it was like the perfect family dinner. We were laughing and playing. We even had the opportunity to talk to my son about the generations in the family. It was really sweet. It was like a perfect evening."

She found Pepperwood to be a grounding force. "On one hand, my family had this devastating experience, but on the other, I could see the land regenerating quickly. Coast live oaks were already putting out new leaves. The trees were scorched, and the fire killed the leaves on them, but then they burst forth with spring green. To me, it's just amazing to witness that."

Michelle also said that, without nature to turn to, people might see the recent fires as thoroughly negative. Seeing Pepperwood, and witnessing the land responding, filled her with hope. "It gives me the sense that life goes on, no matter what happens. Finding refuge and peace in nature is so critical. I wish that more people had more access to natural landscapes. It just shows you how fast we can recover."

As for Arthur and Jill Dawson, they've found losing a home to be a deeply traumatic experience. They've advised potential donors to approach any victim of such trauma not only with open hearts but also open ears. "Ask what someone needs before you give it," Arthur says. "There's a thing called 'receiver exhaustion,' and it's real. So much can come someone's way that even to refuse it is exhausting." The Dawsons have found a temporary home just upstream from their old site while they rebuild.

Although they have no desire to leave the neighborhood, the Dawsons no longer see deep green Glen Ellen as immune to wildfire. As a historical ecologist, Arthur says he should've known better. Because their house wasn't in the footprint of the valley's 1964 wildfire (a previous, slower-moving incident), Arthur assumed they weren't in danger. "But in 1923, fire did sweep down from the Mayacamas Mountains all the way to the valley floor. The winds were so strong that people said they 'couldn't stand against them.' It could certainly happen again, so we'll build our house more fire safe this time."

Back in our Sonoma home a week after our initial evacuation, Paul and I check our phones for the new fire detections. The outbreaks are finally moving north, away from our neighborhood. We camp out without power, cooking on a portable stove on the back porch, watching as the last helicopter of the evening passes overhead. It looks like an army ship, one of the elongate ones with top rotors front and back. It's hauling a tragicomically small bucket of water north toward the latest explosion of fire. An organic farmer who delivers a box of fruit and vegetables to us every week texts after nine-thirty p.m. He's heard that "things are bad" now up at Sugarloaf State Park and Hood Mountain Regional Park. We saw the newer fires from the road as we drove in: the half-dozen or so smoke plumes looked like volcanic fumaroles, pushing straight up and gray, issuing from near the peaks, joining at the inversion ceiling in a flat-topped layer-cloud.

At home, the air is thick and still. Our immediate neighbors to the north are about to leave town—they've been mostly staying in the neighborhood all week. They're "sick of being here." Their pool, unserviced during the fires, is green and leaf-covered. They've stripped their walls of original artwork only to find no room in their cars for any of it. They'll leave the precious belongings behind. They hand us a bag of coalesced, crushed ice, which we desperately need for our coolers.

For a while we run our emergency windup radio, and we pull in an East Indian music station from San Francisco. The sitar is soothing—"wonderful," Paul says. The host's chatty commentary is in a language we don't know, but it sounds like he's making jokes and laughing at his own humor. We laugh with him, letting off stress in waves. When the radio winds down, we are left in a dark house, in a dark neighborhood. The quiet and lack of glaring streetlights suit us. We're feeling peaceful, for the first time in days, even though we're packed and ready to jump and leave again if need be.

I check the sky a few times in the night. There are stars, the hum of a generator far down the street, the absolute lack of glow from porchlights. Quiet woods thick with brush are still fuel-ripe for burning. The morning will break a little smoky, first light greeted initially by helicopter chop and only later by birdsong. The fires are still pushing their perimeters north. The ships are still in the air.

This home we built and had viewed as an island in the madness of burgeoning California is as vulnerable as any. If we hadn't believed until now that firestorm can get into our little oasis, we weren't paying attention. Even if we can't handle it and want to leave now, there's really nowhere else to go. We're all hunkered down in the same refuge.

9.

WHERE THE BIRDS ARE

American Robin

SOMEONE RAPS AT MY KITCHEN WINDOW BEFORE DAWN, and I jump. Who could be visiting so early? The horizon is still emerging as a gray line across the ephemeral lake outside my cabin. I'm not expecting guests at PLAYA, a writers' and artists' residency center in Summer Lake, Oregon, a place as remote as Neverland. Someone knocking at my cabin so early, or at all, couldn't be good. I turn to find an American Robin sitting on an outside sill, reptilian eyes up close to the glass, brittle beak touching it. He taps, pauses, taps again. My pulse settles. Who's afraid of a big, bad robin besides the early worm out in the lawn? Still, the bird's persistence rattles me. I've a creeping suspicion that he's mentally ill. Field biologists I've worked with have said that abnormal avian behavior is a sign that something's gone haywire in a bird's brain.

Later today, Noah—a writer and birder par excellence staying in the next cabin on the PLAYA grounds—will dispel the notion that the robin is psychologically disturbed. Such tapping is common this time of year. The bird is simply failing the "mirror test," not recognizing his own face in the glass. This someone-gently-rapping sees a possible mate or a territorial rival instead of a reflection of himself. It's normal for the robin to disregard the data.

Noah says, "He won't stop until you close your curtains."

I loathe shutting out some of the most dazzling light on the planet, here on the spectacular edge of the Great Basin. From dawn until nightfall, the sun plays tricks with perennial dust storms across the surface of shallow, changeable Summer Lake. Thunderstorms blow up in great, sweeping clusters of murky-bottomed clouds. Every minute brings a different sky.

Still, I shut my drapes so I can get back to work.

During my first residency here, I labored on a novel manuscript sunrise to sundown, as an ant works. The light show over the lake would catch my eyes, and I'd look, but just for a moment before shaking it off. Only in the afternoons, once I'd poured my best hours onto the page, would I go out exploring.

Now I'm using the same method, this time struggling to get something down about water in this basin. There are snippets of dialogue I've overheard, bits of conversation. One longtime resident of the valley has let me in on a few of its water secrets. She says the place is bursting with change. There are rich reserves of underground water here, but people are beginning to worry about its durability. The markets for Oregon-grown alfalfa go far beyond the borders of the state—and beyond the continent. Alfalfa from PLAYA's neighbors goes overseas; European and Asian markets buy up the local hay, grown using precious, ancient water that's been stored underground for many centuries. The community is pumping the aquifer as if it's endless. No amount of natural recharge could recoup the depletions in kind.

So foreign markets take a large share of Lake County's fresh water. Naturally the local humans as well as local wildlife rely on the basin's water too, in a primal, hand- or paw-to-mouth way.

Last year I drove to the wildlife area just once. On the morning of my final full day in residency, after I'd done all I could on the novel, I decided to go birding solo. I drove up the road to where the birds are, at the refuge-not-refuge (technically an "area" because hunting is allowed seasonally). A kiosk at the entrance to the area noted that hundreds of species of mammals and birds live on nineteen thousand acres watered by an elaborate system of pipes and canals. Exciting, the prospect of water, even if artificially moved around. I entered on a dirt road at a breakneck speed of eleven miles an hour, seeing a few ducks and geese. Looking for great horned owls in leafed-out trees, I found a few. Raptors were everywhere: red-tailed hawk, northern harrier, merlin, osprey. At the eastern edge of the property, after a casual left turn onto a dike road, I hit the brakes hard. The promised land! Or promised pond.

Thousands of ducks, geese, terns, gulls, sandpipers, phalaropes, and other shorebirds browsed a shining pond. Some were in flight. Some strolled beaches with their fuzzy, clumsy young. Some dived and dabbled. Some faced beaks-first into the forever-wind, side by side with wooden decoys made in their image. As I scanned the bounty with binoculars, a small gull winged past. Its black head and thick white crescents above and below its eyes were markings of a Franklin's gull. New to me: a life bird. The moment was as sweet as sipping clean spring water.

For this second residency, I've been staying away from the wildlife area, taking the same, focused approach. I got so much done last time! I will again!

But as I face the page, I realize that I've arrived with flat batteries. I'm as drained as the corroded AAs in a misplaced flashlight. How futile to try to work; how amused I'd be if I had the energy to laugh.

Somehow I'll rally. I'll push through the hours. I'll barely leave the cabin for breaks. I'll do as Jack London said he would do (and did): "I shall use my time."

But now, there's this robin. Out past his little head, fields flash with the scarlet and yellow of house finches and American goldfinches attacking dandelions for their seeds. An oriole hops branch to branch in a pine, his orange and black matching the sunrise. Farther west, snowfields sparkle high on Winter Ridge.

People and birds come here pretty much for the same reason—to stop over for long or short stays in a basin with a wide, blue sky and sweet, seasonal water. PLAYA is on the Pacific Flyway, the air route taken by birds traveling between Alaska and northern Canada and points south—mostly via the Klamath Basin southwest of Summer Lake. Some migrators pass through in minutes. Some linger for days or years. A lucky few stay for their lifetimes.

I draw the curtains. An inner voice warns that I need rest, or fresh air, but I push the thought aside. When else will I have this time to work? The planet needs every sympathetic voice now that climate deniers have been voted into major public offices. We're on a fast train headed for a brittle trestle, and I have to help slow the trip.

The robin moves to a bedroom window, where the curtains are still open. Now he uses *that* glass as a mirror. I put on a pair of noise-canceling headphones, which I thought I'd never need out here. The tapping resumes, but at least it's farther away.

A little voice tells me that something could be learned from the robin, but I labor on. Fourteen more days to go.

Common Poorwill

THE NEXT DAYS OF MY RESIDENCY ECHO THE FIRST. RISE, GO to the desk, fill the page with new words. Stop to make lunch, eat while working. Soldier on. At night I seldom sleep, tired but wired. I *persevere*, knowing full well the Latin roots: *per*, meaning "thoroughly," and *severus*, meaning "severe." Thoroughly severe. *To continue with little prospect of success.* Maybe the definition pertains to me, but at least I'm getting some new words down.

On the fourth morning, I review what I've written. My heart falls. The sentences are dead on arrival, not an original idea in the bunch. The manuscript is dull and overblown. In short, it's utter crap.

Crushed, I step out to my back deck as a flock of white-faced ibis, long necks outstretched, pass over the shimmering lake. Noisy pairs of Canada geese bark like small dogs in tall grasses. Migratory birds seem to be arriving in hordes. Last summer, longtime residents noticed a difference in migratory patterns here, "like the migration never ended." Birds continued moving through PLAYA well after the customary spring window for their travel had closed. Noah tells me that migrations do end; the birds get where they're going and stop. They turn around and fly the other direction when seasons shift, but only after they've spent several months at their snowbird-lifestyle locales.

Returning inside, I look in the bathroom mirror. Fatigued eyes stare back from a drooping face. That can't be me. Even my worst photographs look better than this.

I rarely drink wine, and never without company. Rhett Butler impressed me with that philosophy early on: "Don't drink alone, Scarlett. People always find out and it ruins the reputation." The hell with it. I open a Grenache I've brought and down a glass before taking the bottle to dinner in the Commons. Conversation is the last thing I want, but I'm required to eat with the other residents twice a week. It means talking.

In a funk over my failed writing, I sit with the other writers, painters, and printmakers at the big communal table. They're describing their triumphs and the unforeseen ways the residency has been inspiring them. They've been finding their voices. They're glowing. I shovel in my meal, hoping that I can get back to my cabin soon.

As I'm busing dishes, I overhear Noah and another passionate birder, the poet Farnaz, talk about driving up Highway

31 to Sleeping Rock Pass after dark. They plan to look for common poorwills. My curiosity stirs, along with my lifelong love of birding, but I push down the feelings. I must rise at dawn to write.

Before I can exit, though, I talk with a printmaker, B., who's completing a six-week residency. She'd come for a three-week stay but doubled it when another incoming artist canceled. When the space opened up, B.'s work shifted. She'd visited the dusty archaeological caves south of Summer Lake where, in ragged holes in an ochre cliff, she first encountered the oldest human remains in the Western hemisphere: fourteen-thousand-year-old fossil human feces. The petrified offal was discovered near the bones of waterfowl, fish, and extinct camels and horses. The antiquity of the assemblage ignited B.'s imagination. Here were traces of an ancient landscape, only miles up the road from where she'd been working.

Stirred by her new knowledge of old environments, B. dreamed up a process of collecting images directly from the ground. She strapped wooden blocks to her feet before hiking nearby trails and Forest Service roads. After the treks, she removed the worn and roughened blocks and inked them for printing. The results have been both coarse and fluid impressions of the basin's geologic textures.

"I gave in," she says. "When I opened to this place and the people, and let the surroundings transform my work, it made all the difference."

I change my mind and ride into the night with Noah and Farnaz. We drive up the highway to Picture Rock Pass, our windows open to the scent of new things growing. Parking by the side of the road on a cinder-covered pullout, we tread with care, not wanting to crunch the scoriaceous rock any more than needed. We overlook the stunted piñon-juniper forest but don't see much in the dark. We listen for the calls of poorwills. The smallest member of the nightjar or goatsucker family, the well-camouflaged ground nester is hard to find but will answer back to a whistled *poorwill*. Despite their names, these birds don't suck on goats; they catch insects by night. That is, they do until they enter their winter torpidity. Hopi people call the poorwill by a name that means "the sleeping one." Meriwether Lewis described that bird's "dormant state" in his journal in 1804.

Poor-will, poor-will, we're hoping to hear. *Silence, silence,* goes the night. In a minute we pick up the steady advertising call of a northern saw whet owl. A few ring-billed gulls fly above us, mewing like winged kittens. Miles away in the valley, cattle moan, their ghost voices carrying above farm and forest.

But the poorwills remain silent. We stay awhile, transfixed by the symphony of other sounds, then decide to head in. On the return trip, Noah and Farnaz talk about the Punchbowl, an open dish of land among ridges above PLAYA. One resident saw five black bears, all at once, on a hike there last week. A mountain lion, too, strolled in and out of sight.

I vow to go, too. Alone. Surely I can take just one day off from the ten that remain in this residency, in this dry valley where robins attack windows and sleep stays a stranger.

Mountain Bluebird

At dawn, after four hours of actual slumber, I head for the Punchbowl with my writing notebook, binoculars, and bird book. I'm out the door before packing my canister of bear spray, but I go back for it. PLAYA's director, Deb, expects me to return by late afternoon, before large carnivores start their crepuscular feeding.

The day is full of birdsong. Shorebirds call and rise from small, trailside wetlands. Red-winged blackbirds perch on cattails, fenceposts, wires—everywhere—singing their signature three-note song. Snipes murmur all around, from fields of alfalfa and wild grasses. Following a forest service road, I find early wildflowers bursting forth in crimson, gold, and lilac every few feet. Western meadowlarks burble and flee as I approach. A thin cloud cover rests on jagged Winter Ridge in the distance. Soon I come to a broad basin that must be the Punchbowl. The trail continues, though, and so do I, despite new growth crowding the trail and fallen trees blocking the road like gates guarding Oz. The only large trees still standing are white skeletal snags, stripped of their foliage and bark by past forest fire. Climbing up and over barrier logs, I take care not to twist an ankle or blow out a knee with each landing. Even so I scrape both shins through my hiking pants, drawing blood. I push on uphill. So far I've seen no bear or lion sign.

After hours of happy thrashing, I reach a green patch of live woods, mostly ponderosa pine that survived fires that cooked other trees. Cliffs of basalt rise in fractured columns above me. The air is chilly and full of mosquitoes. Busy swatting insects, I nearly miss seeing a bird perched just yards away in the island of green. It's the bluest bird in the history of the world, a mountain bluebird, poised to fly. It's many shades deeper than the sky. Remembering that a story is told in the details, I catch some of the day in my notebook, quick, like floating dandelion seeds. The bluebird hops out to fallen timber and eventually flees.

Down in the valley, buckskin-hued acres stretch in all directions. Verdant, scattered stains of marsh, where groundwater is close to the surface, stand out from the basin's overarching brown. To the north are the ponds and canals of Summer Lake Wildlife Area, pulling with the universal lure of watery sanctuary. Summer Lake, the body of water, has shrunk over the years. Really, it's a *playa*, in Spanish, "an area of flat, dried-up land, especially a desert basin from which water evaporates quickly." In 2017, record rainfall swelled lake levels higher than they'd been in living memory, but the lake dropped back to record lows when it wasn't boosted during the following, droughty winter.

A hay truck drives by on narrow Highway 31, appearing toy scale from this high up. I snap a photo of that one vehicle, the only thing moving in any direction. Later I'll find the picture and wonder what I was trying to capture.

On my way down the trail, the pull of gravity quickens my steps. Midway back, I flush a poorwill from a clump of manzanita in the overgrown trail. The goatsucker rises and escapes on a rush of wings. If only Noah and Farnaz were here to see it.

Back in the cabin, after eight hours of climbing, bushwhacking, birding, and dreaming, I barely have energy to clean up and eat while standing in my kitchen. I fall on the bed and sleep until four a.m.

Nine days of residency to go. It may not be long enough.

Franklin's Gull

AS SUNLIGHT COMES UP OVER THE STIPPLED LAKE, I SIT AND write. I'm remembering the Franklin's gull from last year, a sighting that sent a jolt of energy through me. Seeing the graceful bird winging above a sedge-lined pond in the god-forsaken desert, I felt I'd just touched a live wire—or at least something hot. Thinking of that feeling now, I push away from my desk. I grab lunch, sun gear, water, and optics. I'm going. I need another hit of nature's inspiration. Driving ten miles to the wildlife area headquarters, I stop to read everything posted on every bulletin board and kiosk I can find.

A story emerges. In 1903, sportsman/president Teddy Roosevelt established the first national wildlife refuge in part to protect birds valued for their plumes and feathers. The resulting National Wildlife Refuge System gradually evolved to create "inviolate sanctuary" for migratory birds. After the 1930s, the only decade in historical record that North American drought was more severe than today's, private and governmental entities set aside wildlife areas all over the United States as well—"to reverse trends of degrading and disappearing wetlands" (per the Oregon Department of Fish and Wildlife). People of the time had seen devastating aridity, with conditions made worse by poor stewardship of important habitats: streams, wetlands, forests. Survivors of the drought understood in their bones that protecting our waters helps provide climate resilience, in a time when that phrase hadn't yet been coined. Wild refuge saves both wild and domestic lives.

Since 1944, the Summer Lake Wildlife Area has been managed to benefit resident mammals and migrating birds. Although social media pages about the property show images of men in camo holding semiautomatic rifles and posing for photos outside dinosaur-sized vehicles, seasonal hunting is said to not only provide income but also benefit the area's mission. Small mammals range from Nuttall's cottontails to yellow-bellied marmots. Coyotes and bobcats roam the land. The area is rich in raptors, waterfowl, and upland birds. They all depend on water that enters the refuge via the Ana River, a tiny, spring-fed stream coming in from the north.

Augmenting the Ana's flows are a few smaller springs as well as three artesian wells. Oregon Fish and Wildlife managers are seeing declines in groundwater feeding the Ana's seeps and springs. Some cite decreasing amounts of precipitation and increasing temperatures, which are projected by the state's Department of Water Resources to continue. In addition, subterranean water is pumped locally for residential, business, and agricultural use, as it is all over the West. That same, heavily drawn groundwater would feed springs and seeps critical to the Ana River and the wildlife area if it could.

How the refuge will stand up to the pressures of increased urbanization, growing businesses, and agricultural needs in central Oregon remains to be seen.

I venture onto the eight-mile loop. The wildlife area is deceptive, not very wet looking in the front acres. But the roads travel on the tops of dikes and past irrigation gates, all part of a system shepherding liquid molecules around the place. I reach the pond where I first saw the Franklin's and realize that I'm holding my breath.

Today there are a half dozen or more of the little gulls, drifting aloft as if gravity weren't a thing. I pull out my notebook and write. *Shorebirds in the desert. Water in refuge = life. Climate change = drier refuge. Alfalfa shipped elsewhere = disrupted water cycle within basin.*

It appears I've started writing about things I came here for.

Finishing the loop, I follow signs to the Owl Barn, where I know the great horneds sleep during the day. They're here now, peeking at me with cat-like eyes and ears. I use a zoom lens to photograph them, so their flight distance won't be activated. *Stay*, I will them via telepathic message. *No need for alarm.* They blink and message back, *Are you out of your mind?*

I return to my cabin and work without effort until dark. I don't count the days left in residency.

Calliope Hummingbird

THE DAYS FLY BY UNTIL THE LAST. I CONSULT A LIST I'VE written of target birds I'd like to see while still here. They're species that have eluded me like stars on a full-moon night. Williamson's sapsucker. Northern pygmy owl. Hammond's flycatcher. Cassin's vireo. Red crossbill. Least bittern. The list goes on. Typing up my field notes, I'm anxious about all the lives dependent on the same water depleted by growing irrigation demands.

Later I take a forest service road to Winter Ridge. The well-groomed gravel surface would allow me to drive fast if

I felt like it, but I go as slowly as the (nonexistent) traffic will allow, about eight miles an hour. Maybe I'll see a Williamson's, a life bird for me, up in the high forests. Maybe I'll hear the low calls of owls. Reaching a wet meadow with a small stream, I hear marsh wrens buzzing, song sparrows warbling, and woodpecker species tapping all around. None resembles the start-and-stop, Morse-code rhythm of sapsuckers, so I continue on.

I drive with my windows open, pulling over often, stopping near patches of old-growth forest amongst new growth recovering from logging. The woods smell like sugar and are full of life. A hawk masquerades as a broken pine branch until he lifts wings and flies. A golden eagle dwarfs the telephone crosspole she's hunkered on. A lazuli bunting, really more turquoise than the lapis blue he's named for, hangs out on a log, lazily, as if everyone and his brother wore such brilliant azure dress.

Conifers have been burned or logged here in swaths and patches, stranding hollow snags alongside live veteran pines and firs. A round of tapping eludes me, luring me one direction until I've gone too far, then the other, with no sighting of any kind. It's like a game of Marco Polo, and I'm losing. I circle and circle in the woods, seeing nothing until a northern flicker pokes his head out of a dead tree. He takes just one little look, sees me, and abandons his roost. He's been inside the bleached pine, making all that racket, teasing me. I'm not sure whether to laugh at the clown face or weep with disappointment that he's not my target sapsucker.

I decide to get over myself and continue on.

The last bird of the day is a stunner, a calliope hummingbird feeding in a burned-over patch of woods. The smallest bird in North America, dragonfly sized, it arrives with a flash of violet throat and soft buzz of wings. The bird hovers only a moment before zooming off. My heart beats hard, flushed with adrenaline at the thimble-sized flicker of beauty. It's only the second one I've seen. The first was at PLAYA last year.

The nagging advice I disregarded in my first days here sinks in—this is what I need. This day, this spark, and the other residents who've worked alongside me. Pushing forward with a well too dry, ignoring the life all around, sustains neither writing nor climate activism nor anything else. Without the springs that water this basin and this creative urge, I could no more spin words for a new book than walk five miles into this night on printmaker's blocks.

So it goes with birding and life. You go out calling for a poorwill with no luck, only to flush one the next day after finding another bird more blue than the sky. Seeking out a sapsucker may lead to a tiny jewel of a hummingbird. Searching for water may take a birder to a mess of Franklin's gulls. B. found the way with her printer's blocks; Noah and Farnaz do with their birding; the birds do with their migrations. They do not fail the mirror test, unlike the robin who showed me the insanity of ignoring results.

You don't always find what you're after, but as Farnaz has said, "You never regret going out." Near the roof of a basin that holds light and sky in the same grip as alfalfa and cattle, you open to it. You crunch the data, no matter how it comes to you. You return to the world, again and again. Then, like the birds, you pour it out in your own voice.

10.

Why We Call It Mourning

A September morning, two days before autumn equinox. I'm driving to Point Reyes National Seashore, stunned and brokenhearted. The road rolling out before me is a route away from phones and computers, away from the news I've received of a friend's death. I'd sensed his passing when I woke up around six a.m., although I hadn't yet read the email that waited, still unopened, in my inbox. Somehow, anyway, I'd felt his departure. How do we know such things? From a shift in the atmosphere? Or maybe a suspicion that grows in the silences between conversations with loved ones. After the certainty, when the words have been said, there's a hole in the sky, weather patterns never seen before. When I did open the email, I stopped reading midsentence and left my desk. I drove off into the end of summer, with its profound signs of letting go. I'd devote the day to the search for a mourning warbler, a bird named for the sacrament of grief.

I'd known Bill for forty years. As recently as two months ago, he'd been working as usual, inspiring with his customary vitality and—as he liked to say—pioneer work ethic. His devotion to the campground and boating put-in he owned on the American River was legion. It had been his family's home for decades. He worked on the grounds daily. His practice of raking gravel and dirt surfaces to a fine finish was well known, as was his commitment to instructing others in the art of it. A humble activity for a man who was a fearless river advocate and successful business owner, using the rake still earned the keen-edged attention he brought to everything. Perhaps it bolstered his fight for water democracy. Perhaps it also brought him a Zen equanimity.

Appearances deceive. Even his unique and unfailing fortitude weren't matches for what leveled him. It wasn't a car wreck, as had claimed some of his family members, or an accident on the wild river he loved, or any collapse of his big heart. Nothing but an epic fight with the king of illness did it: cancer, the great equalizer. Struck down in battle with the Big C.

I drive in silence, radio off. The road hums under my tires. *The Big C got Bill C* is my mantra or, as my meditation instructor says, "the primary object." It's a mantra I can't sustain. My mind rebels, violently rejecting Bill's passing. I struggle to get hold of the primary object, but in the spaces between breaths, I despair that the strongest, most vital person I knew could waste away in matter of weeks. A beloved boss to hundreds through the years. A generous friend. A supreme husband and father.

A big, fat lesson in impermanence.

MOURNING: FROM THE OLD ENGLISH *MURNAN*, TO FEEL OR show deep sorrow for someone who has died. Fashion historians claim that the custom of wearing dark clothing to funerals dates back to the Roman Empire, when citizens donned black togas during the mourning period. Some experts say that the custom of dressing up for graveside homage derives from pagan tradition—survivors relied on disguise to hide from returning spirits who might be greedy for more victims. In Christian monastic ritual, official mourners would mask themselves to varying degree in cowls and cloaks. Twentieth-century etiquette prescribed semi-formal clothing for funeral attendance: men in dark suits and ties, women in dark dresses. Victorians set out a calendar for how much and what kind of fabric should cover a widow—black, nonreflective cloth to start, transitioning to fewer yards of material allowed to have a sheen, then further yielding to simpler garb in deep purple. "Widow's weeds" were layered-on, heavy black crêpe, worn for usually more than a year. Extremely small children were not "put into mourning."

Today we can wear what we like to any ceremony, and we do, but we understand the process of grieving better than ever. Ritual serves purpose, helping to move us through the Reconciliation Needs of Mourning: in wearing black or attending a friend's memorial or witnessing a rifle salute, say, we acknowledge the reality of death. From there we move through other stages of grief: observing the pain of loss, remembering the one who's departed, developing our own identities, searching for meaning, and finding ongoing support from others.

Months from now, I'll realize that my search for a bird in a black hood had to be the start of accepting Bill's passing. I don't know it yet, or know exactly what my heart needs, but out of impulse I go to the source—the water that he treasured and defended. He'd been on the Stanislaus and had helped found Friends of the River. He'd seen what could happen. He stayed on the leading edge of fighting dams and other projects that threatened the American River, his home stream. He ran for and won a seat as El Dorado County supervisor. He had a firm grasp of community, technical details of waterworks, and process. As fellow former supervisor Ron Briggs would tell the *Sacramento Bee* in the days after Bill's passing: "Bill always had a full command of the facts. I always hated to argue with him."

But within the first twenty-four hours of his departure, I'll spend the day as Bill might, in his endless capacity for appreciating water. I'll go where warblers sing at springs and creeks.

OVER THE PAST WEEK, MOURNING WARBLERS HAVE BEEN sighted at Point Reyes, their exact locations reported on the eBird and American Birding Association websites. *Geothlypis philadelphia*, the mourning is an American wood warbler, a five-inch-long feathered dynamo with charcoal-gray hood, black bib, and olive back and wings. The bird lives mostly in eastern and central North America, wintering in South America and summering in Canada. Showing up in Point Reyes puts it far outside its usual migratory range. Right now it should be working its way south along the eastern front of the Rockies in good snowbird fashion. Instead, strong northeast winds related to a monumental hurricane season on the Atlantic seaboard have diverted some migrants to the Pacific coast. Perhaps the mourning is one of these windblown birds.

Warblers favor streams, springs, ponds, marshes, for-ested areas—alive places—relying on insects hovering near or hatching from water sources. To search for warblers is to stand among cottonwoods, willows, and oaks, watching with all your might for a flash of color from a small being who's come for a drink or is chasing down mayflies or mosquitoes. With the sound of running water on hand, the pain of the day is at least tolerable, reduced for a moment to background noise.

The last time I saw Bill, he was in lively conversation across the campfire from me at last year's Seder. That annual ritual is when river guides gather to acknowledge the river and friendships. At this one, though, Bill and I never made eye contact, never went around the fire pit to say hello. It was a first. In the decades of Seder, I'd never missed greeting him. We'd always exchanged big river bear hugs and swapped tales about our kids, various enviro-political views, and dreams of what came next.

Last year, each time I'd headed his way, I'd been drawn off course by conversation with other dear friends. I never did get around to him. I didn't say goodbye in person, either, as he was leaving us. I did it through the mail, continuing a years-old, paper correspondence from the days when he was operations manager of the company that employed us and I worked as one of his area managers.

How to forgive myself for not seeing him off? Buddhist instructor Jack Kornfield advises us to seek or grant forgiveness in three ways. Ask it *of others*: please forgive me for not saying goodbye. Offer it *to myself*: I forgive myself for not saying goodbye. Offer it *to others*: I forgive Bill for leaving without saying goodbye. Or for leaving at all.

I scan the trees for warblers. The creek plays its soft music. Blackberry brambles line the bank. Brown creepers dart over Doug-fir trunks. Birdsong comes from all directions but goes silent when a woman walks through with a dog the size of a small horse. Once they pass, the woods stay hushed except for the trickle of water. Morning mist is so thick that my clothes dampen as if dewed by a light rain. Sunlight gleams through a veil of miniscule droplets.

Bill would embrace all of this, if he were here. A sparkle would fill his eyes on seeing the type of green sanctuary he'd always stewarded. He'd shine more still if his whole family was here with him: wife, son, daughter, grandkids.

Song sparrows sing from atop the coyote brush. Chestnut-backed chickadees chip in the conifers. A yellow warbler shows up, canary colored with faint orange streaks on the throat and breast. Anna's hummingbirds buzz before I see them, then zip past with a whir of wings. Another shy bird hops from branch to branch with the light step that comes from being diminutive (just four-tenths of an ounce, the weight of two US quarters). Orange on the face and crown. Blood-orange at the throat. Black stripes on the supercilium—above and around the eyes. Blackburnian warbler! Maybe even more than one. My heart lifts for the first time all day. I forget for a moment that I'm out here in mourning, in search of a bird with a little dark hood.

~

TWO MONTHS LATER, MORE THAN FIVE HUNDRED PEOPLE gather in the riverside campground that Bill owned with his wife, Robin. Beer, wine, and countless potluck dishes crowd four long rows of tables. A flotilla of rafts sits at the shore of the American, ready for the river portion of the ceremony. The water smells of the startling sweetness of leaf decay. There are speeches full of heartfelt and teary memories. One of Bill's brothers-in-law, John Cassidy, voices what many must be thinking: we knew that the grim reaper would start coming for us, but we didn't know that he'd start at the top.

Running water is what links us. We were or are river guides, kayakers, river advocates, Friends of the River board members and staff, rafting outfitters, canoeists, fishing enthusiasts, whitewater rescue specialists, community folk who live in the American River Canyon. Bill was a leader among us, someone who embraced responsibility as soon as he began boating. First he assumed the mantle of head guide without hesitation, while many of us eschewed the extra *hassle*. Later he'd manage the California portion of the company, then its full range of operations. He and Robin married in their twenties, when the rest of us were still obsessing over "keeping our Volkswagens running," as Cassidy quips. In time they owned part of the business—all done smoothly, without obvious hesitation. They seemed to be on a one-way trip to making a permanent move to the river, where they'd bought property. Bill settled early into one place, with one goal: to grow.

I have no notes from the day of Bill's wake, but it's lodged in memory. The phenomenal number of people, all the lives he touched. The moving speeches that invited us to picture the perfect river trip that we hope Bill is on now. Tears and singing of his favorite songs by Leonard Cohen. Boats launching into the winter river; the plunge of Bill's wife and daughter into the frigid water. Their dash for the hot showers. My own remembrance of his advice that we "get naked with our feelings" and my hope that he's on the greatest, most naked adventure of all now. Somewhere I read that the thing that will kill us is already inside of us. We may worry about terrorist attacks, car crashes, and airplane engine failure, and those things are real, but they may not be what gets us. The seeds of our own deaths are already planted, encoded in our longtime experience or DNA. We don't have to look far to know how our lives on this earth will end. As we pray for Bill at the riverside refuge he tended and that his family will carry on, I remember hearing of his ongoing complaints of stomach pain. The shock and not-shock at his stomach cancer diagnosis followed, as did the initial unbelief when it resulted in his death.

But Bill was too strong to succumb, I tell my husband. Paul, who has experience with cancer and its ways, tells me that it's not like that. It's individual to every person it claims. Bill's illness consisted of his own forceful cells, his own passionate life force. Why wouldn't it move fast and be strong? It would have to be robust in so vigorous a man.

LOOKING FOR THE MOURNING WARBLER, I DRIVE TO THE EDGE of land, toward the Point Reyes Lighthouse. Squalls pass over my car, blowing down sheets of rain. My mood has gone as dark as the black bottoms of clouds shredding and reassembling overhead. The light over the ocean shifts from ashen to leaden to blinding white. I'm alive to the cypress groves on either side of the road, attentive to the movement of birds in their branches. I brake for a procession of California quail and take the time to ID hawks perched atop the trees. Later I continue to the parking lot for Chimney Rock, where I gather up my gear and step into the moist sea air.

A man who's eighty if he's a year peers at me as I pull out my pack and binoculars. He asks what I'm looking for. When I tell him, he steps up to adopt my mission as his own. I don't mention that a friend has died and I'm lost; I don't have to. This man named Michael falls in beside me in a makeshift expeditionary force. He's been studying the reports of sightings, too, and points out a road where a mourning has been seen.

We follow the pavement. To our left, Drakes Bay tosses in an onshore wind. Brown pelicans waft in airy queues, while Brandt's cormorants and common loons dive and rise. Michael says that once the road levels out, we may see several different warblers. Small birds flit everywhere—white-crowned sparrows, fox sparrows, black phoebes—but we see no mournings on the lower road.

We change our tack and take the high road, our plan to look down on these same cypress from overhead. We flush a barn owl from the eucalyptus, spot red-breasted nuthatches scaling the cypress trunks like large bugs. We glimpse the elongate body of a warbling vireo as it darts among coyote brush. We listen. Michael uses a portable amplifier to boost the birdsong for his failing hearing, a process that he says eliminates their "sweetness" but at least makes them audible. The rattle of a spotted towhee off to our left, Michael says, sounds like a pile driver.

We try for an hour with no luck. At that point Michael shares news that I haven't heard, that the mourning has also been seen at Drakes Monument. It's a short drive away, to another embayment, another parking lot. He wants to bird the lighthouse, so I head to the monument alone, with an urgency he doesn't question.

Parking near Drakes Monument, I skirt willows alive with birdsong. This is a marshy place, a meeting of fresh and salt water. Slopes thick with woods and scrub rise to bald, grazed inclines. At the base of the hills, an unmarked path leads into a thicket that Michael has described for me. There's a woman already in there, on her knees where the path ends. At first I think she's praying to the granite cross commemorating Drake, two feet from her. Then I realize that she's down there generating most of the bird calls I've been hearing.

Her cell phone sits on a stone beside her, playing back the *chip-chip-chip* of a mourning warbler. When the recording stops, she presses the screen to start it again. In the moments between playback, she *pishes*, or makes small, rasping sounds. Warblers are known to respond, and she must know it, as she alternately pishes, presses her phone for playback, and taps a device on her hip that makes a complicated buzzing call. She keeps up a wall of sound.

The woods are full of birds. One in particular catches my eye: yellow body, charcoal-gray hood, dark eye, black bib. It pauses for only an instant, perhaps drawn in by the artificial bird song, then pops back into the deeper thicket. It leaves as fast as it arrived.

Mourning warbler!

The moment isn't reverent and prayerful or packed with homage. Instead it's tarnished by all the pishing and chipping and warbling going on. This method of birding isn't uncommon, but I've never seen such an egregious example of—well—impatience. After a few moments watching the woman in utter fascination, I leave the thicket.

Michael pulls into the lot beside my car. He extracts himself limb by limb from his driver's seat, slowly, deliberately. He asks what's going on in the thicket. When I tell him, he frowns. He marches toward the monument with as much strength as he can muster. I follow, to back him up if nothing else.

It turns out that he knows the noisy birder by name. They strike up a conversation. He's concerned, he says, that corvids (crows, jays) will follow her birdcall into the thicket and raid the nests of the very songbirds she's calling. She argues, albeit politely, that she'd never pish during breeding season. Still smiling, she gathers up her things and leaves.

Quiet descends. Michael turns up his audio device. Two more birders find their way to the monument, and they're all eyes. Various warblers dart through the trees, lower and lower, like descending leaves. Michael whispers that he's seen black-throated blue warblers here, and we all redouble our scanning of branches and boughs. A bird flits far overhead, an individual that might be a MacGillivray's warbler.

Then, in an instant, the mourning warbler comes back. He pauses for just a moment, but he's so close I could reach out and pet him. I take a long, unashamed look. He's an immature, with only a hint of dark hood, reminding me that funeral attire is perhaps not for the young. His presence here takes my breath—a thousand miles from home, a vagrant on his way south. That this little spring-fed copse offers him temporary refuge on his journey fills me with unearned pride: the Left Coast Sanctuary State. With climate so wonky now, bird species that have lived with hurricanes for millennia need as much high-quality habitat for stopover as we can muster. This place has it.

AT SEDER THIS YEAR, I SIT WITH BILL'S WIDOW, ROBIN, ON A stout wooden bench beside the river. It's an hour past sunset. The water is pewter colored, restful to the eyes. Our conversation is interrupted at intervals by a ruckus of Canada geese making flyovers, some skidding to stops nearby. It's April, the eighth month since Bill's passing. A friend of Robin's who had lost a child had warned that the seventh month following her loss would be the worst. Indeed it was, Robin says, for reasons she can't explain. Maybe the transforming fire of grief changes our physical selves, similar to the total replacement of cells our bodies undergo every seven years.

Robin has faced a mountain of learning. Tackling the family finances. Learning to deal with endless bureaucracies. Facing ongoing bereavements, like the moment she's heading home and there's no one to call to say she's on her way. Noticing the scream of the red-tailed hawk on her own, when before she'd always shared it with Bill. We observe each small thing as we watch the river go dark.

I remember the time I saw Bill catch a spider in his kitchen, with a small Tupperware bowl and a square of cardboard. He smiled as he did it, his full attention on the arachnid, his movements careful. This man who was building a riverside business from a dusty dirt lot, who'd kayaked countless streams, paddled oceans, and hiked miles of trail, put as much care into trapping one small being as he put into mentoring and loving his family, defending rivers, and overseeing hordes of employees. He let the spider go free in his garden.

Now when any living thing can't find its way out of my house, I grab an empty cup or jar. In gentle increments, I trap the creature under a dome of glass or plastic. If it's a moth, it may dart end to end in its three-inch prison before it rests. Meanwhile I'll slip a magazine over the mouth of the container and carry my prize to the back door. Outside, the woods may be alive with the cleansing scent of bay tree. The tops of redwoods may be swaying in the wind. I'll lift the magazine to let the being go. It will fly on, to somewhere I can't see.

In the morning I'll rise early to leave the American. Driving Interstate 80's stark pavement will be the inhospitable route to Paul and my own creekside oasis. A Bullock's oriole whistles atop a cottonwood; acorn woodpeckers cry and tap wood. Meanwhile the calls of California quail remind me that my first week of training to be a guide took place here, on the banks and currents of this very river. I went on to an obsessed career of professional rafting with the same company that had led me to Bill. As the covey of birds calls and groups up in the underbrush, my friends from Seder have risen and are drinking morning coffee on boulders and benches beside the water. It's a contemplative, streamside refuge, part of the legacy that

Bill left us—the immense gifts his daughter Rebecca identified, with heartbreaking accuracy, at his memorial.

I begin the drive home. When I get there I'll be chasing migratory vagrants again, at this time of year headed north. The coastal refuges will be full of life. If I ever see another mourning warbler, or even if I don't, I'll think of the American, the sanctuary for river travelers Bill and Robin created with unswerving love, and the journey we all must take when we leave it.

11.

WIDOWMAKERS

IN MY HEADLIGHTS, DAMP ROSETTES IMPRINT THE BRIDGE across our narrow creek—literally, *Pequeño* Creek, or Little Creek. Muddy paw prints track the dusty steel plank in a dark, chaotic trail. Some creature must have climbed out of the water just before I drove home tonight. The animal trundled the width of the bridge, dipping back into the channel on the far side. Maybe the same creature left the smudged, five-fingered marks I found on our side door yesterday. In their rare forays onto our porches, animals lean on the glass, the pads of their feet pressed toward the inside. In past years it's been mostly raccoons, masked visitors, chattering as if we'd left off some prior conversation that they're just picking up again. Their soft, brown eyes peer into the interior, looking for something. Stray cat food. Scraps of bread. Food items we never offer.

Raccoons, though common, aren't the only strangers to come by our door. We've often glimpsed the hunched backs of other animals on the move. Raccoon. Fox. Bobcat. They cross our property on their way to Pequeño Creek, most frequently in the spring. We've looked for the berry-rich scat of fox and listened for the sharp hoofbeats of does and fawns on wooden decks. We've seen oversized, high-haunched bobcats moving through tall grass and up into the hills. Mountain lions sometimes rest in the shelter of an unmowed yard down the street.

Animal sign was more common here before the drought: splayed impressions in the stream mud, scat packed with a hash of crawdad shells. With changes in the neighborhood—drier landscape, more fencing, new structures—hazards have grown and visits dropped off. Wildlife are scarcer on this quarter acre overall; perhaps with our ephemeral creek going dry for longer, the animals' need for water pushes them farther in search of ponds, reservoirs, and larger, year-round creeks. When I see raccoons now, it's usually by the side of the road, dodging cars in hunchbacked flight, or already struck down and lying lifeless on the shoulder. Drivers zoom by, oblivious to the carcasses, so common.

Still, creatures do come to the creek when it flows. Trails like the one I spotted this evening can be found if we look. More often there's the unmistakable smell of death, the sign that a fawn has perished, abandoned when a mother has met her end on the road. Sometimes the smell persists, and we can't find the source of it.

Lately a neighbor, who claims to have an excellent nose, tracked down one of these death scents. She led her husband to the middle of decking they'd just finished installing and pointed to boards that had been nailed down only days before. The scene was something out of a TV drama, where a psychic leads investigators to a body: "She's buried right here."

A raccoon had died under the freshly mounted two-by-fours. "It must've crawled under there and then couldn't get out," the neighbor said. "I hate to think that it suffered."

THE BLAZING HOT DOG DAYS OF SUMMER HIT LIKE A SLEDGE-hammer. There is nothing subtle about them. Not named for the lazing about of overheated canines, rather the days have roots in Sirius the Dog Star. Between July 3 and August 11 in the Northern Hemisphere, Sirius rises with the sun. Greek and Roman people believed that the combined incandescence of Sirius and Sol brought on summer's stultifying temperatures. These days we know that Sirius is too far away to blame for the heat. Instead, the tilt of the Earth's axis alone, which moves us closer to our sun, brings on the so-called dog days of midsummer.

In my town, summer brings families out of their homes and into the public pools. One of these, which draws its heated water from natural hot springs, also draws me. In the locker room, conversation usually starts or ends with reactions to the weather. In true California fashion, the range of temperatures considered comfortable is narrow, between seventy and eighty degrees Fahrenheit. Some like it hotter; some like to talk about it. "It's freezing today" (when it's sixty-five degrees); or, "that wind is vicious" (when it's gusting to fifteen miles per hour); or, "you're brave to be out there" (when swimmers have used the outdoor pool on an overcast day where temperatures have dipped into the forties).

On the dog days, though, especially in extended heat spells, conversation turns to how to stay cool. Open up the house at night and close windows and doors in the morning, before temperatures climb into the nineties and hundreds. Close drapes and shades before the sun hits the windows. Of course, there's always forced air: "this heat is what air conditioning is for." Conversation usually doesn't turn to wildlife and birds, but when it does, some swimmers observe that wild animals don't have AC.

Reactions to this truism vary. One woman whose answer I recall best simply shrugged. "Oh, well," she said. "There's nothing I can do about that."

WILDLIFE BIOLOGIST GEOFF PRIDEAUX FINDS HIMSELF IN tears when he remembers the February 2018 fires on Kangaroo Island, southwestern Australian. "Our community is about four or five thousand people. A very small community, and we have a seasonal tourism of two hundred thousand, in the summer." February is getting toward the end of summer Down Under, wearing through both tourist and fire season. When the third big fire of the year hit in February, volunteer crews mobilized at once, as they always do. Geoff's wife, Margi, also a wildlife biologist, worked dispatch during the fire. She acknowledges the predominance of natural fuel that surrounds their home. "Around our farm is quite a lot of national park, which is all dense eucalyptus with a number of seasonal rivers that run through. And where there's not national park, there is plantation timber, which is eucalyptus again and paper products and farming community."

The native plants are "highly, highly flammable," Margi says. "The eucalyptus and our grasses might as well be matches. Their tendency to burn is part of the psyche." At dusk on the first night of the fire, ninety-five crew members were out on the ground. Every single one was a volunteer from the community. "In rural Australia, that's the fire crew," Margi says. "Sadly."

Sadly but proudly. "We knew we had to hold the fire ground," Geoff says, "because if we'd lost it, the fire would have gone into uncleared scrub and forest, and it could've been catastrophic. So we just thought about holding a spur that was to the west about a mile or more from where we started. Flames were roaring up the hill. It was blowing debris into the air. It was getting difficult to breathe. We couldn't see half the time, either, because the wind kept swinging on us, and it kept blowing into us, so we were pretty tragic by the time we finished, pretty sooty. Eventually relief came, at about 1:30 in the morning, because we couldn't leave until someone else showed up, and we had to stay or they wouldn't have known how to pick up the ball."

Geoff and team drove up and down hills for hours, protecting residences, helping people defend their property, refilling the truck at farm ponds. All the people he encountered were from the community. "These are all people we know. It's a very personal thing. Everyone was heat exhausted, everyone was in the same boat. But we kept going because we were protecting our fire ground for our community's sake."

It's not the agonizingly long hours that Geoff put in fighting the fire that brings him to tears. Rather, it's the personal side of his story. "One of the dams that we were pulling from to fill our truck was a writer's residence. There were guests there, a family—a mom, dad, and three kids. The crew and I were getting pretty thirsty for drinking water, it was hot, and getting supplies up to us was tricky, because nobody in their right mind would come up to where we were just to drop off some water and some food. It's dangerous. You have to drive right through the flames." Geoff and team filled up at the guests' house, observing when they did that the family's only protections from the fire were four in-ground front lawn sprinklers.

"They had the sprinklers madly going. They told us that some other appliances [water vehicles] had already saved their house once. Now they were keeping their eyes out for any bits of flying embers that could possibly flare from somewhere else."

Geoff had long ago run out of drinking water for himself and his crew. He admitted to being "kind of in shock." He'd brought a couple of empty bottles and asked the guests to refill them. "They came back out with a whole pile of full bottles that completely packed the front of the truck."

Margi says Geoff can't tell the story without sobbing. "These little kids," she says, "and the whole family were so thrilled to be able to do something to try to say thank you. They were unprepared for the fire, and they were watching other people put their lives on the line, and there was this human spirit that just wanted to say thank you in any way they could. So that was a beautiful moment, this family bringing these armloads full of water and ice cubes. That water kept the fire team going for another four hours."

Geoff and Margi were also moved for another reason. With wildlife as their expertise, they're aware of the huge losses to the animal populations that must have occurred. "The big animals, like kangaroos and wallabies, are able to escape the fire. Some don't, some get trapped and die, but most of them are able to escape because they can move quite fast. The smaller things that can't mobilize that quickly, like possums, die in the fire. Probably the koalas aren't able to get out of some of the gullies quickly enough.

"The big loss, of course, is one of the island's endangered species, which is a black cockatoo. Its key feeding habitats were burned to the ground, and it's got very little feeding range left now. The wildlife people on the island will probably put replanting programs in place to try and overcome it. But it's a bird that we can't artificially feed, because it has a limited diet of the nuts out of a particular kind of seedpod on a tree that doesn't grow often. So it will be a big loss, but no one's calculated it yet. It's a pain that you don't want to deal with, because there's almost nothing you can do."

IN SUMMER HEAT, WILDLIFE DOES ITS BEST TO TAKE CARE OF itself: move into cool stream corridors, find shade, find water. Summer is also baby season, with young wildlife more at risk in the heat than their parents, because babies can't always do anything to avoid the sun or overheating. In the wild, for instance, young birds can climb from a nest onto a branch to cool, but if they're being raised in owl boxes or other unnatural shelters, they get trapped. Once they're in a box, they can't always get up and leave.

Monitoring the boxes we've installed is critical. So is checking our backyards to ensure wildlife movement. In rural counties, backyards are part of a larger landscape. As temperatures continue to rise, animals move to cooler coastal and higher-elevation regions. Allowing them passage through fencing and protecting open space are ways to help them deal with extremes. Often a homeowner who builds or buys a new house immediately fences the perimeter, which blocks movement. Gaps can easily be left, or smaller spaces fenced, allowing wildlife to pass.

We don't often think of our properties in terms of whether they hinder animals moving to water, but we can. Night-lighting and noise should be minimized if they're keeping wildlife from feeling safe near water sources like creeks, ponds, and fountains. Plantings can encourage better water-holding qualities in soil—native plant life often does this better than exotics. Native species evolved with the birds of a region and so offer appropriate food sources.

And what about preparing for the fire that threatens entire populations? Controlled burns and clearing work best, and managing flammable undergrowth through prescribed fire and thinning. Preparing forests for the epic fires to come gives wildlife—and us—a chance.

WIDOWMAKERS ARE "THINGS WITH THE POTENTIAL TO KILL men." Married men, I gather. A technical reach of rapids on the Stanislaus bore that name; both the rapids and the name gave boaters pause. Widowmakers, to foresters and loggers, are branches and trees that fall exactly wrong, killing as they crash to earth. Geoff Prideaux describes widowmakers as "full-grown trees that are completely on fire, where pieces can fall on you."

"It's embarrassing," he says.

"And dangerous," Margi adds.

Fire in general has a vast potential to make widows, orphans, widowers, and bereaved parents of many of us. So, too, does summer heat, as more days climb into triple digits, and people and wildlife all over the world cope with additional heat- and water-related stresses. The same loss of habitat that limits animal movement in hot weather now also hurts them in terms of sheer living space and diversity.

"We've seen huge declines in biodiversity," says Mary Ellen Hannibal, author of *Citizen Scientist: Searching for Heroes and Hope in an Age of Extinction*. "Over the last forty years, we've lost twenty-eight percent of the world's vertebrates, thirty-five percent of butterflies and moths, and 1.5 billion birds. This is happening in our own backyards, not just Africa, not just Asia, but right here at home." Growing heat kills individuals, threatens fledglings and young, and simply decreases water availability and the extent of water-dependent habitats.

In addition to habitat loss, lack of precipitation in drought years contributes to wildlife decline. Even with normal or wet winters, extreme heat in the dry season increases evaporation at our reservoirs and raises demand for irrigation in fields and gardens. Groundwater and surface water are essential to the native habitats like creeks and wetlands on which wildlife depend. The lovely natural landscape that attracts so many residents and visitors thrives on the same sources we do.

Protecting open space for wildlife migration and preserving native habitat for food and water availability will remain critical strategies for stewarding our wild neighbors. Having room to move is important to wild animals.

"It's the old story of when you build it, they'll come," Hannibal says. "There's no way to overstate this—we have to protect wild nature. It will take a group effort. It's a mob source thing. But the good news is, there's still a lot of wildlife left, there's plenty to save, and when you provide habitat, they come back."

For Margi and Geoff in Australia, it's a matter of not only protecting their own wild nature but also making sure the adjacent wildlands are managed well. The February fires happened at a time when the dams were still full—water availability wasn't the issue. But they did have a lot more tall grass due to some lingering rains, adding fuel to the fire. The rain-driven overgrowth and the lack of managed care on the ground by newcomers intensified the already high fire risk. "Originally the allotments would have been in farmland or goats or sheep," Geoff says. "But new owners in the community had done no grazing, so the grass grew tall. The terrain is steep and awkward, so much so that you can't get a truck in to slash the grass or do other fire preparation."

Margi says it's a new thing with the community, that the people who fight the fires are usually the large-share property owners. "We're the people in the trucks, out on the ground. But if the fire breaks out in an area where a new element or type of community member has moved in, who are not fire conscious, they allow growth around their dwellings, they plant things close to their homes that are not safe, they don't have any fire break around their houses. There's contention in the community about that. Because people are putting their lives on the line, and there's a feeling that the people who you're going out to protect could've been more careful about the way their properties are managed.

"So that's going to be a whole new conversation that this community hasn't had before."

THE LESSON IS THAT WE CAN STEWARD OUR OWN PROPERTIES, no matter how large or small, to protect against heat and fire.

We can keep our gardens wildlife friendly. Reducing stressors to wild animals helps them when the heat climbs. Each gift to them becomes a gift to ourselves in the surprising sights and sounds of nature. Learning about wildlife passage, how it connects livable space for animals whose survival is linked to ours, opens our hearts and minds. Applying essential principles to our own yards makes a difference on a micro scale during the hottest days. Every little bit counts; every act is both a gesture and an incremental contribution to the whole.

We can conserve water like lives depend on it. Whether or not we're in an official drought emergency, we're on a trajectory toward hotter and drier. Creeks and rivers are wetted from underground flow from the water table, which can be drawn down by overuse. We can be mindful of that use every time we come to the tap: these pipes connect to my river.

We can be kind to distressed wildlife. We can expect more animals around fountains, ponds, and yards in the summer and allow them the room. Wildlife follows instinct and will move on once a heat wave is over. No need to panic. Some animals, like raccoons, that are otherwise nocturnal may be out during the day. Know whether they're showing signs of heat distress (long tracked by Australian and other websites) and open up access for furry and feathered water seekers as much as possible.

We can build simple birdbaths. Clean water is important in most gardens, especially those open to birds and wildlife. Birdbaths help small songbirds especially, as do fountains with a slow enough trickle for birds to wade and splash about in. The National Audubon Society posts easy-to-follow bird-safety instructions on their website. Why not help those whose habitat is most at risk? It takes little effort on our part, other than opening our hearts.

Any action that creates refuges in our homes and lives is so much preferable to simply concluding *oh, well*. We're better than that. Aren't we?

12.

THREE DAYS TO BE HERE

"THE LONGER THE TRIP, THE MORE HEALING OCCURS." So
says my friend Peter Winn, geologist and Colorado River
guide, about the therapeutic effects of whitewater trips through
the Grand Canyon. "Change happens for people almost without exception." The most dramatic transformations he's seen
have been in disabled military veterans on sixteen-day kayaking trips organized by a group called Team River Runner. He
has more stories than he can count about the river's ability to
restore. "One army communications expert came home from
Iraq so full of shrapnel, he'd lost his ability to do even simple
math and would only say 'fuck you.'" By the end of the trip, he
was giving eloquent speeches of appreciation for the canyon
and his fellow boaters. Later his wife wrote to thank the crew
and the river for getting her husband back. This supposedly
hopeless case became a Bureau of Land Management river
ranger in Oregon. He found his place.

Another Team River Runner veteran, a helicopter mechanic
and copilot in Iraq with shrapnel in her brain that couldn't be
removed, came to the river feeling suicidal. Peter learned that
she'd been in and out of hospitals and therapy for three years.
She didn't want to kayak, so he taught her to row his raft. "She
did so well that about halfway down I just gave her the oars
and rode on other boats. She ran all the rapids without flipping,

then went home and got into competitive road bicycling. She just won a major women's race in Europe."

I too worked as a Grand Canyon river guide in the 1970s and '80s. The job, the place, the people, the lessons—all were seminal, watershed experiences in my life. The river, and that river especially, threw its arms around me and put behind the awkward years of high school forever. Once the river had me, I found it easy to recognize the same love affair happening for other people on the fourteen-day trips we led. Passengers made the trek to our rafts at Lee's Ferry, Arizona, from all over the world, escaping deadlines, responsibilities, and overflowing voicemail and (back then) paper-filled inboxes back home. I became an expert in knowing just when someone would forget about life above the rim. As the river took them through legendary whitewater and to hidden grottoes and waterfalls, the rock walls got taller and the canyon experience deeper.

Author and Colorado River guide Louise Teal, independently of Peter and me, saw the same sort of changes in her decades of guiding. "After three days, the passengers and the crew can really *be* on the river. People not only heal physically down there, they sometimes change their lives. They get or quit jobs, marry or divorce. Or they become river guides themselves."

Peter agrees that three days is about par. "But it takes some people longer." When it did, he'd work to ease any discomfort. "As a guide, I often singled out people who were slow to get into it, invited them on my boat, and tried to make friends with them." They'd relax enough to really arrive in the sanctity of place.

Then the place worked its magic. The canyon may appear vast and overwhelming when seen as a whole, especially when viewed in the mere seventeen minutes the National Park Service notes as the average tourist's visitation time to the rim. What the mini-visitor doesn't grasp in that time is the pockets of sanctuary tucked everywhere in the canyon's recesses. Deep green waterfalls. Pockets of shade and cool. Pools in red rock. Ferns, monkey flowers, cottonwoods, willows.

"You only have to get them there," Louise says. "The rest is cake." Get passengers to the river, earn their trust, and take them deep into what she calls the "zillion-year-old rocks." She and I were passengers before we took up guiding. Then we never wanted to be apart from the canyon's soul-stirring sunsets, embracing rock walls, and endlessly flowing water. Those we guided, too, found it a beautiful, intense, and, in Louise's words, "completely fulfilling place." It is—a place out of time, out of overwhelmed mind.

So take me to the river. Drop me in the water.

GUIDES KNOW THAT RIVER TIME IS GOOD FOR THE HUMAN body and soul; the physical mechanism behind how it happens is less universally agreed upon and understood. The science of nature's healing had been little researched until 1982, when then-Secretary of the Japanese Forestry Agency, Tomohide Akiyama, coined the term *shinrin-yoku* ("forest bathing") to describe the practice of getting into nature for body and mind renewal. By then the tradition in Japan was already ages old, but putting a name to it went hand in hand with making recommendations for how best to achieve nature nirvana. One should walk, sit, gaze, and exercise among greenery. If hot springs are available, one should immerse in them or another water feature. All five senses should be engaged during practice. One should even eat well-balanced meals of organic, locally sourced food, according to tradition.

That mud bath your river guide is recommending? Take it. You'll engage your tactile, olfactory, auditory, visual, and sometimes even gustatory senses. Inhaling the scent of a desert sage, the aroma of sediment in the water, the feel of warm sand on your toes—just what the doctor ordered.

When Akiyama recommended forest bathing those many years ago, he knew about the pioneering studies of phytoncides—basically pungent essential oils—conducted in the 1920s and '30s. The oils, volatile compounds exuded by conifers and some other plants, reduce blood pressure and boost immune function, among other benefits. More recent research has found evidence of twenty-one "causal pathways" to improved health, all falling under the umbrella of enhanced immune function.

The pathways are chains of nerve cells and sequences of chemical reactions. They're supported by the footpaths we follow into forests, on hills, through canyons, and on rivers. Nature provides the soothing sights and sounds, health-boosting negative air ions, and decreased pollution and heat we need for good health. We respond with increased awe, greater relaxation, restored attention, and improved vitality. The health outcomes are astounding: enhanced production of anticancer ("natural killer") cells, reduced cardiovascular disease, fewer migraines, lowered anxiety—to name only a few benefits of simply getting outside into a natural setting.

It's not just our imagination that we feel good when we brush up against nature. It's good science.

IN JAPAN, ALL FIVE SENSES ARE TO BE ENGAGED DURING shinrin-yoku practice, preferably in certified Forest Therapy Bases that are well maintained, embraced by the local community, and possessed of health-boosting qualities. To be considered therapeutic, a qualifying forest must show a measurable decrease in stress hormone levels in practitioners. As part of ongoing base certification, forest bathers undergo blood-pressure and stress-hormone analysis before and after wandering in the woods.

Therefore most data we have about nature's benefits is derived from monitoring shinrin-yoku subjects. Much of the peer-reviewed science has been done on northern temperate forests, such as those in Japan. We also have good data about our response to water and the seashore, according to Kathleen Wolf of the University of Washington College of the Environment. "We know less about response to tropical environments or desert environments." Which begs the question of how well we do at an oasis that lacks a central pool. What we do know is that we feel good out there, a notion firmly supported by science. Among the research are studies showing that spending just three days and two nights in nature increases the immune system functions that boost feelings of well-being for up to seven days afterward. The same amount of time in a built environment has no such effect.

What we'd intuited to be true in the canyon is borne out by results of measuring stress hormones in the semiwild.

That the three-day phenomenon well known to river runners is supported by science comes as no surprise to my friends and me. We've seen the escalating love of kayaking, rafting, canoeing, duckying, and surfboarding with a mix of understanding, delight, and dismay. River running is so popular now that many of us who once had rivers to ourselves can't get permits. Demand for what began as an arcane wilderness experience has burgeoned since its beginnings in the 1950s and '60s to the point where river recreationists in the United States compete for a set number of put-in dates. Private river permits are managed by resource agencies through highly competitive, web-based lotteries. Similarly shinrin-yoku, once known only as such in Japan, is growing in popularity in the West. Trainings for certified guides, taught all over the world, fill well in advance despite sometimes-steep certification and membership fees.

Likewise, nature and water immersions are prescribed more and more by health professionals. For my friend Susan Karle, a California-based Certified Forest Guide and long-time Licensed Marriage and Family Therapist, reconnecting with nature for her own personal and professional lives led to applying it to help her clients. Nature was important to her growing up, and she returned to it because of the seriousness of the issues in her work with victims of trauma and abuse. She found that simple daily sits under a giant live oak in her yard helped sustain her.

"Maintaining my best energy was the big motivator. A few years ago, I took my first guided nature walk and found it so powerful that two weeks later I signed up for the five-day training to be a Certified Forest Guide in shinrin-yoku walks."

These days Susan's outings begin with a sharing circle in a shady meadow, where some participants express a hope to reclaim the freedom and happiness they'd known as children playing outdoors. Others have been feeling stressed and need time out from responsibilities. Susan may invite everyone to find stones to hold their worries for the day, then to toss them into a nearby creek. Choosing and discarding worry stones is one of "literally hundreds of techniques" tested by the Association of Nature and Forest Therapy Guides and Programs (ANFT), which trained Susan. M. Amos Clifford, founder and director of ANFT, has found about forty techniques that he calls keepers, "meaning that they work very well."

Susan believes that people are willing to try shinrin-yoku right away because of the solid research behind it. "And they see that it's been effective for me." The initial impulse that leads people to seek help, though, is a desire to feel better. In many cases, she recommends nature. "In Japan, doctors and other healthcare professionals have prescribed forest immersion for a long time. We're finally doing it here."

One of Susan's clients had a huge trauma background, involving the death of a family member, leading to a crushing sense of isolation and depression. The client thought she'd need years of therapy, but being in nature with a trusted group helped speed her process. "With shinrin-yoku," Susan says, "she reconnected to feelings of hope and goodness, which had gone out of her life. She graduated from therapy in less than a year. When she said she felt she was done, I said, 'Yes, I think you are.'"

When I first arrived at the Grand Canyon to work as an assistant guide, I met Wesley Smith. Eight years prior, Wesley had been drafted and served as a foot soldier in Vietnam. He'd grown up in Williams, Arizona, sixty-three miles from the canyon. Once in the army, he'd asked to go to southeast Asia after hearing that it was "pretty casual, not much going on." The year was 1968. He was sent to the Mekong Delta two weeks before the Tet Offensive. The company he joined had 130 men, he told *Boatman's Quarterly Review*, in an interview published by Grand Canyon River Guides in Flagstaff, Arizona. He left the company after eight months. "We had gone through 520 men to maintain a 130-man strength. There were like twelve people, six, two, somebody killed every day. Sometimes hundreds of people stacked up."

Out of sheer will, Wesley stayed alive and helped his buddies survive, too. As he says, once you're over there, there's no way out. "If it was in South America or something like that, you could walk home. But you can't swim across. There's nothing that you can do except go out there and say, 'Well, I'm going to do what I can do. I'm going to protect my brothers, and I'm going to try to kill as few people as I can, because it's for no reason.'"

When he did get home in one piece, he vowed never to work again in his life.

His brother, though, worked at a filling station in Williams. When guides from Arizona Raft Adventures (then American River Touring Association) came through to buy gas, they said they needed an extra hand on the river. Wesley's brother got him the job.

Wesley knew the canyon from hiking in as a Boy Scout before the Colorado was dammed at Glen Canyon. "Underneath the bridge at Phantom Ranch, where the nice little lagoon and stuff is, there used to be these big sand dunes, and it used to be that real silty mud." He and the other scouts avoided the mud, but they loved the swimming pool at the ranch. "We wouldn't get in the river . . . but the swimming pool! 'Yeah, let's go!'"

When Wesley was asked to help guide, he knew nothing about rafting. He pictured coal barges or other big, serious craft. The guides who'd recruited him said, "No, you take people down on boats on vacation."

Wesley said, "Uh-huh."

He found his first trip "like going into the Bible or something . . . I looked at it and I went, 'Wow, this is just so neat!' I was just so happy to do it. And I never thought that I would be asked back or anything." But the company came up short staffed, and Wesley worked the river again. He found it "just incredible. I'm sure it's like that for everybody. And there are places in the canyon that I haven't gone, that I don't go, that I save for special events."

His aversion to the muddy water changed with time. He saw firsthand how diving deep into the river experience helped people to really arrive during their first tentative days in the canyon. He allied with mud as he never had as a youth. He had a knack for getting people into impromptu mud baths at the confluence with the Little Colorado River. He'd just lead them in. The natural tendency to help others he'd showed in Vietnam didn't fail him. A few days into any trip with Wesley, people would roll on the mucky river bars, coat themselves from foreheads to feet in slick mud, bask in the sun, and become one with the earth. Then they'd float downstream in the clear, blue Little Colorado and wash away the mud. They'd get cleaner than they'd ever been in their lives. Any thoughts of staying pristine with scented, store-bought products fell away. So did the limits of the circumscribed world.

Wesley passed in 2000, after working more than two

decades on the river. I still miss him with a surprising fierceness. He had the most wondrous gift with people, although he stayed a bit of an enigma to many of us who loved him. The river—his sanctuary—wrapped him in its arms for as long as he could stay on it and in it, and he paid forward that huge embrace.

TIME IN THE FOREST, IN THE PALM OASIS, IN THE GRAND Canyon—it's much more than a neat little pause in which we put away our devices. It's not just a nature cure. That sense that nature stands outside of us is a philosophy that prevails mostly in the West. Eastern-based mindfulness practices and meditative traditions have long aligned more closely with human oneness with nature. Indeed, there's an evolutionary component to that oneness to which the East has no prior claim. We evolved with nature—in it and around it and among it— and we depended on it. As Kathleen Wolf says, "We had to rely on our senses, our intuition, and our responses in order to find food, water, shelter—the absolutely important things. We hunted or grew our food; we carried it back to the tribe."

Kathleen says that we evolved a microbiology on our skin and in our gut as well—our microbiome—that's important to health and wellness, including even mental function. The immunity-boosting bacterium *Mycobacterium vaccae* abounds in forested and mountainous areas; human exposure to *M. vaccae* prevents serious depression, suicidal thoughts, and chronic immune dysfunction. So, too, does immersion in an environment ripe with biodiversity: being in nature with a variety of species has been shown to be critical to acquiring essential skin and gut bacteria.

Research is growing about children who don't get sufficient dosages of nature early in life. "They do not develop proper immune functions to protect them as they get older," Kathleen says. "To be in nature is to ingest those things that set up a healthy, thriving microbiome." With the sterility of some of our cities, with no parks and no trees, children don't get an adequate dose of nature and are set back from the outset. "They're not on a level playing field. Access to nature is critical to thriving populations."

Colorado River guides know the value of nature, especially around water, as a critical part of our physical and mental lives. As shown by the Wounded Warriors, as shown by Wesley and the scores of hurting people that he and every river guide ever led into nature, even unimaginably traumatic situations and hopelessness may be healed when we reclaim our connection to source. As Peter Winn says, "For decades I've believed that I'm part of nature, not separate from it or 'above' it. Many years ago I studied Zen Buddhism and learned to meditate. Eventually I found that just hanging out on desert rivers had the same effect as meditation—no stress."

There are those who call shinrin-yoku a prescription to counter our modern obsessions with technology. Others say the trend toward being outside in nature is a fitness fad. I say whatever works. If getting out into those zillion-year-old rocks and hidden grottoes does it, then go. You have to do what will keep you alive.

13.

EVERYBODY WAS SO NICE

ONCE UPON A TIME, I WANTED TO WRITE A BOOK ABOUT water and storytelling, and I wanted to go to Canada to do it. I'd had the impulse for years, long before the 2016 US presidential election, when one hundred thousand Americans helped crash the Canadian immigration website overnight. I was not one of those people, because at the time I'd just adjusted to being back in California after living north of the forty-ninth. My supporters, the US Fulbright Association and Fulbright Canada, had warned me about the potential for culture shock when first visiting a host country and also when coming home. They'd sent out that caveat as part of their orientation packet. I'd read the warning and assumed it would never apply to me. How difficult could it be to visit an English-speaking country and ally just a border crossing away? Neither did I anticipate facing challenges in returning a year later to the town where so many people knew me that I called it home.

After all, I'd been to Canada once or twice. They hadn't minded my visits before, even when I was on foot, aimless, and carrying a backpack, guitar, and umbrella. How accepting, when I had no job waiting anywhere, only seasonal work that had just ended, and no plans other than to ride the Canadian railway to visit a friend in Terrace, British Columbia. True, my last visit had been a lifetime ago, but it had been a breeze. The immigration and customs agents had smiled, asked to see all the traveler's checks in my wallet, and sent me on my way. They did say "eh" and "sorry" a lot, as I'd been told to expect, but I found those expressions charming. Now, with an invitation to the country from respected organizations in both Ottawa and Washington, my going to Canada would be easier yet.

Not so. The young customs agent in Windsor, Ontario, eyed my passport as if it were written in Cantonese. He squinted at the letter of introduction from my hosts. Naturally, it was his job to question me—he had to fill out a form that lay on the counter between us, and I wasn't fitting into the boxes he had to check. He had never heard of Fulbright anything in either of our countries. He squirmed when I described the nature of my work.

"So you'll be writing about water," he said. "What about it?"

"About the way it's used in ancient and modern storytelling."

"Sorry. Go sit down."

My husband waited with his brother Mark and sister-in-law Jen, who couldn't stop grinning. The situation reminded them of sitcoms they'd been watching lately on TV. "If Larry David could see all these uniformed officials in flak jackets not letting a writer into Canada, he'd have a field day of it." Mark and Jen had driven us from Ann Arbor and hoped to take us on to our lodging in downtown Windsor. We'd all begun wondering how long this would take.

Some time later the agent called me back, asked another question, and told me to sit again. Then he waved me to the counter for more inquiry. This went on for the better part of an hour, me scurrying between his window and the visitors' chairs. He'd frown, wave me away, and go discuss my answers with someone behind a windowless door. He'd always shut it behind him, disappearing for up to ten minutes each time.

He'd had no issues with Paul, who had a guitar in a gig bag slung over his shoulder. When asked, Paul had only to say he was a guitarist and music instructor. The agent handed him back his passport with no questions and no worries, but then gave me somber instructions: "If he plays in bars and such, he needs to not be a repeat performer and not under contract." What, he was encouraging him to work under the table? Paul didn't like to do that even at home.

The agents detained only one other visitor while we waited, a disheveled fellow pulled from a chaotic line of bus travelers. The others off the bus had been breezing through the turnstiles like they were entering Disneyland.

"What do you have in your backpack?" the agents asked the unwashed fellow.

"Clothes."

"Where are you from?"

"Texas."

They had him open his pack. He pulled out crumpled clothing and piled it in a heap. The agents picked through shirts, trousers, socks. After they were finished sifting his belongings, the traveler repacked everything and moved on. In his wake, the agents joked in low voices. "Only two things come in from Texas." They laughed. Neither clarified what the two things were.

Finally the young agent attached a work visa to my passport with a resigned air. He took no pleasure in allowing me into his country. Maybe the stress of safeguarding borders in a post-9/11 world had gotten to him. Or the usual fatigue at the end of summer tourist season. It couldn't have been my considered proposal about the critical nature of storytelling in understanding water issues both north and south of his border.

As Paul and I headed across the road to exchange currency at a cash window we'd been eying, another agent flagged us down.

"Stop!" she said. "Where are we walking to? We are not to walk there. We are to return to our vehicle, back up and turn around, then proceed out the right-hand side of the gate." *We* did as she said. *We* take well to being reprimanded as if we're small children who've disobeyed some set of clear instructions.

Or as if we were an alien species, as I'd already begun to suspect.

I'D APPLIED TO WORK IN THE WILDEST PART OF NORTH America: British Columbia. I'd been part of decades of researching surface water and groundwater in Northern California and had become obsessed with why we scientists had failed to engage our community in meaningful conversations about our work. We'd given talks, hosted forums, presented data, posted graphs, and published papers, newsletters, and press releases. Yet we'd failed to impart to people how rich our region had once been in fish and healthy streams. We'd also fallen short of communicating that remnant populations of steelhead trout could still be found right here at home. How we used water mattered to the creeks and sloughs that the fish traveled.

Our local news outlets had rocked with public outrage when a group of unsightly, chainsaw-sculpture bears were installed outside the local Black Bear Diner. And yet reactions to our articles about water use and fish presence in local creeks created little or no ripple of commentary.

Why not? Why weren't people picking up on this stuff? Around the time I started asking this question, I met Kendall Haven.

Kendall is both scientist and storyteller. A former employee of the Department of Energy, a consultant to organizations ranging from the Environmental Protection Agency to the National Aeronautics and Space Association, he claims that he's "the only West Point graduate to ever become a professional storyteller." In 2005, he began a relentless unearthing of information to show that science outreach succeeds best if presented in story form. He'd been making a case for changing how NASA shared its data. The public would never understand what the agency did, Kendall argued, unless it took an entirely new approach to communications. A director at NASA's headquarters wasn't convinced.

"Prove it," the director said.

Kendall dug in to find proof. He expected to uncover only hearsay and anecdote. Instead, he struck gold. He was overwhelmed, he writes in his book *Story Proof*, "by the mountains of available, pertinent, qualitative and quantitative, research-based studies" that support storytelling's case.

So what defines a successful story? It's best told as "a detailed, character-based narration of a protagonist's struggles to overcome obstacles and reach an important goal," Kendall writes. Story that is effective and compelling—and above all memorable—incorporates eight essential elements: protagonist, character traits, goal, motive, conflicts and problems, risk and danger, struggle, and details.

"Stories happen on the ways to goals," Kendall says. Without the character's goal and the motive behind it, seasoned by conflicts and risks she must struggle past, there is no story. Without story, only one to two percent of information and images any one of us receives will have a lasting effect on us. So Kendall discovered. "You do not vividly imagine them in your mind. They do not engage you on a deep emotional level. You do not remember them."

If I wanted to change the world through good science, I'd have to put it into language and images that people wouldn't forget. The massive pile of stream and fish data I'd worked hard to acquire for a good part of my professional life could help shape the future of the West and, if extrapolated out, the world. Information had no value, though, if no one knew about it or acted on it.

Deciding to bet my career on story as substance, I went to Canada on a mission for water in the West. I had a goal of my own: to find a story to tell.

FULBRIGHT ASKED ME TO REPORT TO OTTAWA BEFORE GOING to work at my assigned host institution, the University of Alberta. What about the Wildest Part of North America, where I'd proposed to set my story? Sure, Ottawa was full of culture and fine food and historic buildings with colonial roots, and Alberta had the prairie and mountains and big rivers, but I wanted to bypass both stops and begin my real research. Our first full day in Ottawa, though, a thunderstorm blew up with epic drama. It was a tempest, really—violent, windy—with phenomenally tall clouds climbing ever higher above menacing, murky undersides. The dark sky roiled. Overdone, like special-effects cumuli. I expected to see tornadoes whip past the Parliament Building, followed by storm chasers gunning their SUVs around city buses.

Tornadoes occupy an unknown horizon in my mind, the way earthquakes inhabit those who don't live with them. There are pilots who fly into the eyes of hurricanes and men and women who drive the interstates toward cyclones rather than away. I'm not one of those people. As a river guide, I learned to pull to shore and wait it out when the wind blows so hard that sand and small rocks start flying. Still, beginning in Ottawa, the weather in the North American interior became central to my research.

Dust and leaves blew up in the wind. Umbrellas whipped inside out, dragging people along. The acrid smell of ozone filled the air with the first flashes of lightning. People ran to escape the inevitable rain. I was inching along, walking with a fellow Fulbrighter, Margaret Moss. A bad knee slowed her progress, so we took our time. While we headed for a tour of the Parliament Building, she gave me a crash course in how to talk to people from other cultures about their storytelling.

A Native American and scholar of indigenous life, Margaret shared her own family story. Her mother had died of complications from diabetes; her sister had been killed by liver failure. One brother had suffered a fatal motorcycle accident; another brother had succumbed to HIV/AIDS. A brother-in-law had been murdered. Several aunts and uncles had passed at early ages.

Margaret's story was so tragic, I figured she must be an anomaly. She'd thought so, too, until she found that her family fit right in with Indian Health Service statistics.

First Nations populations of Canada are "at risk," she said, "and the risk is treated as if it's inherent in the populations themselves. Really, it's the process of that group interacting with the world that puts it at risk." First Nations women are murdered at ten times the rate of the next-largest group of violent-crime victims. Other abuses—rape, battery—are also higher in indigenous families than other groups in the nation. Most of the crimes go unprosecuted, not even hitting the "big charts," Margaret says, because the incidences are considered "statistically insignificant." The average life expectancy of a First Nations male: thirty-eight years old.

My gut sense was that water played its part here. Maybe it's the first lens I turn on the world, and I always return to it, but this sense proved true in the months of research to come. First Nations people inhabited areas where streams and food sources were being contaminated, often by mining and drilling. Oil, gas, metals—all had huge environmental costs that affected the people who hunted and fished Canada's waters for a living.

Margaret and I and our cohort eventually reached the Parliament Building, where a royal grandeur filled every space. A hush lingered in hallways. The storm drama moved west, growing smaller outside the oversized windows. Everything inside the government chambers loomed large, from the remoteness of the ceilings to the width between walls. A guide toured us around, pointing out the international flavor of the rooms. Paneling and floors made of exotic woods had been stained, polished, cut, and milled to add to the general elegance. So ironic that the governmental center of any country should be embellished with wood and stone from foreign shores, but it's common.

The parliamentary baseboards were the exception. They were pure Quebecois bedrock, ancient igneous and metamorphic stone from the Canadian Shield that underlies most of the eastern provinces. On that rock, the French and British fought each other for control of the continent, with the aid of native allies. Countless lakes sit perched and sparkling on black-and-white gneisses and schists that have seen it all. The four billion years of geologic time represented by the stone put my six months for research in perspective. Time would pass before I could catch my breath.

Regarding water and story, lack of time isn't only my problem. It's everyone's.

AT THE NATIONAL GALLERY IN OTTAWA, I STUMBLED ONTO an outsized Kwakwaka'wakw transformation mask in the museum's Canadian Hall. Encased in a plexiglass box, suspended so it appeared to be flying, a carved eagle held a green, black, and red killer whale in its talons. The fish was ten times the size of the bird, and yet the eagle was managing to carry it. How could it be? An interpretive sign shared the story. A village was starving, so a young man transformed himself into a raptor and traveled to the ocean to fish. He nabbed a killer whale, flew it home against all logical size and weight restrictions, and saved his people by sharing the catch. Naturally, there was a hitch. When he went to change back to his human self, he couldn't entirely lose the eagle form.

Maybe in taking on the raptor's persona, he'd defied

tradition. Maybe using magic wasn't allowed. Or maybe he'd just become so changed in making the hero's journey that there was no going back. Whichever was true, he had to live with the consequences of assuming superpowers. Exile is the reward for many great heroes who've given their lives to the cause, and he was one of them. He wasn't embraced again by the village. Whoever said that "no good deed goes unpunished" could have written this story.

The mask had hinged jaws that opened and closed to reveal the wearer's human face. Any observer would know that there was a man in there, even disguised as the raptor he'd become. In that superlative detail, the mask embodied change. The act of transformation was memorialized in the carver's skill using nature's materials to craft moving parts.

Months later I would learn that a transformation mask this massive (five feet long and two feet tall) had to be borne by the central wearer along with two attendants. It reminded me of the dragons I'd seen during Chinese New Year in San Francisco, where a costume covered the backs of many dancers snaking down city streets together. Collaboration. Coordination. Ceremony. And yet the man who wore the eagle mask also learned the loneliness of the long-distance flier.

I raised my camera to photograph the eagle mask. Immediately a guard rushed toward me, pointing to a *No Photo* symbol plastered on a wall ten feet away. Hadn't I seen it? It was about the size of a Canadian dime—no, smaller. I hadn't noticed it at all.

After Ottawa, I was off to Edmonton, Alberta, where I learned some key ingredients about the province from reading the news, looking at maps, and talking to as many people as I could: (1) the weather was extreme, as it always had been, but was becoming less predictable; (2) the economy rose and fell based on how much bitumen (a hydrocarbon pronounced *bitch-*

you-men) could be extracted from the *tar sands*, or sandy soils in the far north; (3) some of the biggest tar sands projects lay along three of the province's main river systems, the Athabasca, North Saskatchewan, and Peace; (4) the prairies were suffering intense lack of precipitation that on maps looked like a milder, northern extension of the severe drought ongoing in the western United States; and (5) the people who found themselves in the most vulnerable situations with regard to Alberta's water and energy politics were those in its forty-five First Nations in three treaty areas and 140 reserves.

The first, second, third, and fourth elements felt like old home week; the States had all those issues and more. For years, in fact, I'd worked on them and little else. The fifth ingredient, though, was not in my wheelhouse. As the maps and narratives suggested, a storyteller couldn't talk about water in North America without diving into the work of indigenous people. It had always been so in the States as well. Weren't Native Americans shunted from the best, well-watered homeland onto dry, desolate, unwanted patches of earth? In my own Sonoma Valley, colonists had rounded up Miwok and Wappo from their homes along streams. They'd either outright murdered the original people or sent them to slower deaths from disease or overwork in Mission San Francisco Solano. The modern-day example of bringing an oil pipeline through reservation land in the American Dakotas doesn't stray far from this tradition— we're invading your valued watersheds. If you want us to pay, we've got cash.

The response: "You can't eat money. You can't drink oil."

In Canada, with its vast underground supplies of hydro-carbons, some of the most embattled cultures are the Cree and Chipewyan and Dene in northern Alberta and Saskatchewan. The tiny, remaining enclaves of subsistence hunters and fishermen have been thrown into battle against the multinational, infinitely funded corporate machine. A geologist I know once observed that Canada was the only first-world country to mine and drill with third-world panache. Environmentalist Bill McKibben agrees. He's called Canada "wildly irresponsible" in aggressively exploring for oil when we can already reach four or five times as much of Earth's carbon as we can safely burn.

At the University of Alberta, professors and researchers are grappling with the province's choices about the environment. The University's College of Humanities introduced me to the word *petroculture*. Taken strictly from the Greek *petro*, it could mean "stone culture," but in current use it marries the *petro* in "petroleum" with *culture*, as in "the customs, arts, social institutions, and achievements of a particular nation, people, or other social group." The college's After Oil vision for the province and country is an organizing principle—if we stopped brutalizing the boreal forests and the populations who depend on them, who could we be? Tar sands, the most carbon- and water-intensive method of oil extraction in the world, won't last forever, but can we outlive it?

Currently bitumen is mined both at the surface and using a forced-steam extraction method that emits more greenhouse gases but, on the face of things, destroys less forest. "Oil companies say they are searching for ways to extract deep bitumen using more eco-friendly processes," Peter Essick writes in a *National Geographic* photo essay shared in *Imaginations*, the university's journal of cross-cultural image studies. Most striking to me among Peter's images is one of a northern forest, beautiful and emerald and windswept. The treetops are so in sync with each other, so perfectly symmetrical, they take our breath. Their delicate, filigreed texture could simply be stared at all our lives, while their spectacular canopy shelters important work and a busy world of breath and oxygen and critical uptake of food from the soil. The forest in the picture was uncut as of the date of the photograph (2009) but had already been claimed by prospectors. By now it is surely gone, scooped up and spirited away to our insatiable appetite for mobility.

Tar sands mining scrapes up trees and topsoil in a process that might as well be scorched-earth leveling. Using hydraulic or electric shovels, operators cut tar sands from the mine pits in bucket loads weighing up to one hundred tons. The dug material contains only seven to thirteen percent bitumen by weight. Such digging eliminates every living thing on the earth's surface and excavates down to two hundred meters below grade. Once mined, oil sands are mixed with water to produce slurries that can be gravity separated to extract pure bitumen. If the product is poor quality, it's upgraded into synthetic crude oil; if it's high quality, it's purchased directly by refineries.

The industry claims that the enormous pits they leave are restored, but only a fraction of the massive scars have been. Extraction is just going too fast. Pits are left to sit, no longer forest, no longer biodiverse nature, no longer producing oxygen or preserving carbon in the ground.

Managing editor Sheena Wilson, who alongside co-editor William Anselmi oversees *Imaginations*, tells me that her son can't breathe at times. They've made trips to an emergency room in downtown Edmonton, sometimes on black-ice nights. His inability to get the oxygen he needs from the air is more than metaphor for an endangered planet; it's a very real danger to her child. It's something we all face.

But the Alberta tar sands are out of sight, out of mind for most of us, and convenient to recast as epical—the triumph of the will over habitat. It's a trope of Canadian literature, Sheena points out, where "What was monstrous/ugly is now rendered as beautiful/entrepreneurial."

Epical. "Heroic on a grand scale" per the *Oxford English Dictionary*, but first seen in the Greek word *epikos*, for "word" or "song." The stories we tell of the hero who journeys to faraway places end in his saving the world. Few but the workers directly involved with the tar sands are seeing them in anything other than photographs. We at the end of the supply pipelines simply know that our vast appetites are being met. How cool is that?

And therein lies the rub. Because if it isn't enough that the lives of wildlife ranging from woodland caribou to lynx are tied to the boreal forest, so is the very survival of the Dene and Cree people. So are all our lives, hitched to the breath we get from the stands of conifers and undergrowth and mossy ground cover that are being rolled back like area rugs from the surface of our planet.

IN WRITING WORKSHOPS, WE OFTEN TALK ABOUT THE RISE and fall of the three-act narrative arc in fiction. We discuss classic examples of the arc, usually from fairy tales or movies or books we read when we were young and still retain in happy memory. *The Wizard of Oz*, Hollywood style, provides a great case study for the narrative arc. In Act One, Dorothy yearns for freedom and adventure and gets more than she bargained for when the inciting incident (story kickoff) arrives in the form of a tornado. When she steps into the full color of her dreams, she's passing through the first plot point to begin Act Two, her journey on the Yellow Brick Road. She gets to Oz, meets the Wizard, and seems about to meet her goal. Then, after all she's done for him (Kill the witch! Get the broom!), she learns he's a fraud and she's never getting out of there.

But hallelujah. In Act Three, she reaches a climactic moment in which she learns she's always had her own power to get home. She goes, and there's a brief winding down, or denouement. She's where she always wanted to be.

We who want to communicate well can learn a lot from Dorothy's creator, L. Frank Baum. Not from his racism, which puts us off him forever ("Why not extermination?" he asked about the Native Americans who were holding on during Baum's heyday in the early twentieth century). His 1900 novel *The Wonderful Wizard of Oz*, with a story line followed faithfully enough in the 1939 movie, provided a model for thirteen subsequent novels. He wrote to "please children," and he used story to do it. His work captures our hearts.

As Kendall has said, "Effective outreach writing (or teaching—or communicating in general) comes from inserting those very attributes of story that scientists think they are supposed to write out." This is a scientist talking.

The story stays in memory. It treads the arc of our evolutionary imaginings. The details of the characters' lives eclipse anything we try to commit to memory from textbooks and research journals. The protagonist striving toward a goal over the course of her narrative arc leads the way to a communication mode that works.

FEW PEOPLE I MET IN EDMONTON HAD GONE TO THE TAR sands, but I did. Paul and I drove to Fort McMurray in a driving rain, then I joined a bus tour that took me into a rippling landscape of hills. I couldn't help feeling excitement, like we were off to see the wizard. We ascended a bluff, topped it, and pulled into a dirt turnaround on its scarred surface. Our guide stood to read us the tar sands corporation's scripted Terms for Photography. Visitors were welcome to take pictures but were not to publish them without written permission. "This restriction applies to books, articles, blog and social media posts, slideshows, websites, posters, conference abstracts . . ." The list went on. The other guests studied the camera functions on their smartphones. No one objected to the terms. We'd soon be seeing the oily deposits that had earned the name tar sands. "But to be accurate, we call them *oil sands*," the guide said.

To be accurate, or just to sound cleaner? I didn't ask.

She held up a stack of business cards as if selling tickets. "Just call our media relations manager with any questions." I didn't wait for a card but stepped off the bus as soon as the driver opened up, out onto ground that was soft and wet. I moved with the caution I always feel near steep drop-offs that could easily precipitate a fall. Miniscule pockets of forest had been left standing. Rain had darkened everything. Contrasts popped: dark brown of dug earth, whites and golds of a few remaining aspen, deep green of conifer. Down below, a mud road climbed an immense ramp. To where? The road ran up a tall, bare slope to nowhere, a horizon with endless sky.

From beyond that horizon, dump trucks emerged. They looked as big as China and carried loads of black earth, perhaps the bitumen the guide had mentioned. As they came nearer, a line of empties passed them going the other way, ascending a ramp and shimmering with mirage waves, although it wasn't a hot day. The empties reached the end of the ramp and— disappeared.

I raised my binos. The outgoing trucks looked like toys at the edge of the world. Trucks driving out of sight, tiny before they vanished. Maybe this place rivaled the Grand Canyon not just in numbers of tourists, as I'd heard it had lately, but also in its immensity once you got to the rim.

The disappeared trucks had to be grinding down the inside of a vast excavation, dropping down some alpinist's highway, downshifting, trying to maintain traction, entering a pit of constant noise and grime. From our vantage, though, we couldn't see into the monster's guts. We could only see trucks drive off what looked like the end of the Earth.

The other people on the tour were snapping photos. They clicked away at the trucks, roads, rutted shoulders, and aspen. When we returned to our seats, no one spoke. They checked their phones. Even the driver had stopped chatting. One couple gazed straight ahead with thousand-yard stares.

LOOKING INTO CLIMATE AND WATER NARRATIVES IN LITERature, I stumbled again and again onto drought discourses from other disciplines. One of the most compelling was a 1997

Australian review article in the *Journal of Sociology* identifying drought as an exceptional influence on that continent's identity. Part of the national character dwelt in the overwhelming length of time they'd learned to go without rainfall. Part, too, was the massive amount of physical space covered by their extended drought. They had done a preponderance of storytelling about "the dry." They storied it as natural disaster, sure, but it was *their* natural disaster.

"We suggest," sociologists Philip Smith and Brad West write, "that discourses cannot overemphasize the significance of water-related natural disasters because to do so would be to threaten the established basis of Australian national identity." Bushfires and extended periods of little to no rainfall not only distinguished the country from its European and British roots but served as a mythology that pulls people together. Communities only act, Smith and West found, when their experience is sunk into story and song. Whether in bush poetry, romanticizing life in the outback, or in aboriginal songlines that map the history of the interior through millennia, the drought narrative owns Australia.

The opposite is also true. Were it not for folk idioms and mythologies that make natural disaster accessible to various groups of Australians, Smith and West argue, megadrought wouldn't be comprehensible to the general public. Cyclones and flooding followed extreme drought in the national consciousness and took out communities. The water-related disasters simply had to be translated "from the raw to the cooked" to be clear.

Interpretation by artists of all ilk is critical to understanding and living with extended disasters like megadrought. So say the studies of Smith and West. "This reflexive turn [artistic expression] is essential if we are to develop rational policies with respect to the range of environmental problems that will threaten Australia into the next millennium."

We in the American West haven't accepted the sort of identity that would lead to sustainable policies in water sustainability. After all, we haven't yet embraced the dry. We're still in *Cadillac Desert* mode, using whatever water it takes to create the faux oasis. We still make unending plans to irrigate no matter how many rivers go under the knife for it. Canada, too, with its shrinking glaciers in the Rocky Mountains, decreasing amounts of precipitation, threatened water supply, and rampant forest fires still carries forth with its wet nation identity. The May 3, 2016, wildfire that forced evacuation of eighty-eight thousand people from Fort McMurray and leveled 2,400 homes finally registered Alberta as a member of the fire-prone West. For one brief, shining moment.

What would it take to get drought into the national discourses both north and south of the forty-ninth parallel? The answer, I am certain, is story.

THE TAR-SANDS TOUR DIDN'T STOP AT THE "UPGRADING FACIL-ity"—we just cruised past it at a crawl. The guide winked at me and said, "You'd call this a refinery in America." Ah, yes. Pipes, tanks, emissions stacks, and bare earth. Back home, refiner-ies like this sometimes explode in random blasts that take out entire buildings in seconds. Or so I'd heard from a geologist who'd safety-checked a facility one day and watched it blow apart the next. The shock of it still showed in his eyes.

We toured on, to an exhibit called *Giants of Industry*, with excavators the size of tyrannosaurs sitting in separate fenced areas. A mammoth tire, four times my height, served for photo opportunities, and the cameras got busy: pictures of the tire with and without humans, pictures of the driver ignoring it, pictures of signs for the washrooms and vending machines.

I waited near the bus, and the guide found me. "You know, we had another American here earlier this month." She named a famous actor.

"Did you meet him?"

Newspapers I'd seen in Edmonton had reported that the actor had planned to "tour the sands." Sometime after that, he'd taken this same bus ride, followed by an overflight by private plane. The guide's eyes darted to mine, then away. "The corporation assigned our most experienced guide to his tour, a beautiful young lady who dressed to the nines, had her hair done in a French roll, paid for a manicure, everything. Then he showed up looking like he just fell out of bed. And his questions! He asked how she could even sleep at night."

"What'd she say?"

"The same thing I would have." Her eyes flashed. "'I'm proud of the corporation. And proud of my country.'"

The tour rolled thanklessly on. We watched a film on the bus's overhead monitors—vistas of forest, marsh, prairie, and rivers of clear water. Ducks skidded onto sunlit ponds. Serene bison grazed a distant hill. "Welcome to Site X," the narrator said, "one of the first reclaimed tailings ponds in the history of the oil sands." The corporation was leading the world of energy into a secure and safe future.

A crew of employees, mostly First Nations women, had planted trees in the facility's waste, in the Site X holding area. A system of ADA-compliant footpaths ran through it. To make perches for raptors, the crew had turned dead cottonwoods roots-up at strategic locations around the tailings.

The narration purred. "Since restoration, the site's toxicity has declined by eighty percent. Workers have seen a ground squirrel, two coyotes, and small flocks of ducks. The wildlife is coming back."

Hope flared in me like a match to a pilot light. They were restoring ruined land? Who could find fault with that? Scientists had figured out how to strip off overburden—a technical name for soil and vegetation—and could roll it back into place like a rug. Once replaced, the forest floor would take root and flourish again. Everything would come back "as nature intended."

We pulled into the Site X parking lot just as the film ended. I leapt off, hoping to get to the pond to see any birds before they took flight. The other tourists followed. Behind me, I heard the others break into fits of coughing. Then so did I. Air like acid rain, without the rain.

A man, part of the couple who'd sat on the bus in shell shock, pointed with a thumb at an upside-down cottonwood. "I've never seen a single bird land on those things," he said. He wore a wide-brimmed, SPF-infused sun hat. "And the trees they planted haven't grown an inch in three years." He and his partner frowned and looked over their shoulders. The others were still some way back.

"You know those blasts we've been hearing?" the woman asked.

"No," I said. On cue, something exploded across the road.

She said, "They're supposed to keep ducks out of the ponds, because if they land on them, they die."

I took a good look at the unrestored water across the road. Scarecrows stood all around the scummy surface. They were dummies with arms and legs bent at odd angles, like prisoners shot trying to escape. Their clothes sagged, too, everything fitting them as if their real clothes were in the wash.

"It's all toxic ooze," said the man, glancing back at the bus. "Thousands of birds have landed in it and had to be destroyed. Have you heard about it, in the US?"

"Not a word."

"But it's national news here—I thought it'd go worldwide."

We kept on, crunching over gravel, until we came to a wooden hatch in the pathway. Stepping over it, I didn't think it strange; but then I remembered that trap doors aren't frequently found in trails.

Later I would learn that a university faculty member and friend of Sheena's who'd been on a specially arranged tour had raised the hatch cover and taken one, quick look. Down underground, a tangle of metal pipes and ducts hissed and clanged. A stench-cloud hit her face. She dropped the hatch and covered her nose and mouth. A worker in a hardhat and blue jumpsuit charged toward her.

She'd peeked into the belly of the beast. Or behind the wizard's curtain. The pastoral scene supposed to be a restored wetlands required a fully engineered waterworks to keep it alive.

LAST MONTH I RAN INTO KENDALL AGAIN, THE FIRST TIME I'd seen him since the lecture I'd attended in 2013. I told him I'd been talking up his research. I had shared his findings at the University of Alberta and at conferences and programs all over the West. He was still collecting data, and he'd found even more evidence weighing on the side of storytelling and the eight story elements. I asked him about the value of the narrative arc in memorable communication. He said the two were indeed linked.

"We're finding, though," he said, "that the story climax isn't always acted out by the protagonist. So we're calling the character who effects the moment of greatest conflict the *climax* character."

"Is she always changed by the moment of climax? As in, she's never the same again?" As in, Dorothy finding the power in her own feet?

"Not necessarily. They just go through that incidence of greatest conflict, and then the story winds down."

I went to Canada; I visited the tar sands. I wrote a novel about them. I came home. But I'd seen what destroying the green forest looked like—the life-giving oasis we all need, the source of our survival. I'll never forget it, as we never forget a good story. Like the one about the eagle who chose to fly to the sea and tried to come home again. He couldn't do it. He couldn't lose the beak.

14.

Fountain of Fountains

B<small>EFORE SUNRISE ON</small> D<small>ECEMBER</small> 29, 2017, <small>NINE BIRDING</small> zealots (including me) meet in the back parking lot at Dunbar Elementary School in Glen Ellen, California. Many in our group have gathered on or around this date for the past thirteen years. We arrive in ones and twos, with sack lunches, binoculars, spotting scopes, and bird guides. The small talk and shuffling feet to stay warm in the pre-dawn cold are part of our annual routine. We're here, as usual, to tally bird species for the Sonoma Valley Christmas Bird Count. Today, though, there's an unusual sense of trepidation as we go through our standard drill of arranging carpools and catching up on the past year.

This Christmas, more than any time before, we're not sure what birds we'll find. October's wildfires raged through this part of Sonoma County, north of San Francisco Bay, devastating both wild and human habitat. The blaze that would soon be named the Nuns Fire snaked through Glen Ellen after midnight on October 9, 2017, missing this schoolyard and several surrounding properties by alley widths. The rest of the town wasn't so lucky. Gale-force winds driving flames before them razed some parts of the rural neighborhoods and circumnavigated others. Dunbar Road, where the schoolyard sits, is a street of blackened foundations of homes alternating with untouched estates whose very survival makes them desolate. A lane of pain.

Over the weeks since the fire, homeowners have been sifting through the ashes near isolated chimneys and on concrete slabs. On one corner lot, a house lovingly built by friends of mine is simply missing, burned along with the stand of eucalyptus surrounding it. Their historic barn was spared. We all speculate: the slate roof saved it, irrigated vineyards acted as firebreaks, defensible space around the barn made the difference. We can only guess, though. Maybe it was that last hosing-down, maybe not. Maybe nothing anyone did or didn't do can explain the checkerboard of burned properties on this road. In any event, the batten-and-board outbuilding among the coals is nothing if not forlorn.

Who would live in this firescape?

INTREPID BIRDER DAVID LELAND LEADS US THROUGH OUR assigned area, the Trinity subarea. David is the veteran of some forty-five Christmas Bird Counts (CBCs) and has been the Trinity group leader for the past several years. During this last week, he's scouted ahead: exploring up steep roads into the hills, scanning the shores of farm ponds, reaching out to landowners by phone. He hasn't been encouraged by what he's seen. "Some places are pretty bombed out," he says, "with almost no bird activity."

Trinity is one of nine subareas within the Sonoma Valley circle. Established in 2005 by lifelong bird enthusiasts Tom Rusert and Darren Peterie of the nonprofit group Sonoma Birding-Sonoma Nature, the Sonoma Valley CBC encompasses 113,097 acres of mountain, valley, marsh, and bay land. It's one of over seven hundred circles around the world. The idea is to pull in a combined dataset that takes a snapshot of global bird life.

Persistent, long-term data is valuable under any circumstances; this year in Sonoma, the data will matter even more. Last winter was a record rainfall winter that soaked the valley and created ephemeral wetlands. It was also an above-average year for the Sonoma Valley CBC, with 77 bird species in the Trinity and 164 in the valley overall. We remarked at the time that we were seeing the valley as it must have looked in former days: pocket wetlands sprinkled throughout, overflow from creeks breeding insects critical to birdlife, rampant growth of woodland shrubs and herbs. A green Sonoma.

When the dry season arrived, that green turned brown in a hurry. It's the California way. The Nuns Fire that raced into Sonoma County (and Napa) hit 8,172-acre, chaparral-rich Trinity hard: 93 percent of the subarea burned, compared to 0.3 to 51 percent in the other eight Sonoma Valley CBC subareas. First raging as a "firestorm" pushed by dry Diablo winds, then continuing as slower ground burns for twenty-four days, the Nuns Fire killed two people in their homes and a firefighter in a water-truck accident, destroyed one thousand structures, and scorched 57,000 acres of urban and wild habitat. That the birds we knew could survive it seemed unthinkable.

The fire also threatened all the Trinity birders' lives and properties; to a person, we evacuated. By some stroke of luck, none of us were injured or lost homes. "We talk about it daily, what could have happened," says Anke Snow, who's birded the Trinity for the count since 2005. Her home wasn't in danger, but her eight-year-old son couldn't breathe the smoky air. They headed for the coast and waited for the all-clear signal. Still, Anke doesn't think of wind the same way she used to. "I regularly have fire dreams. Not fun."

NUÉE ARDENTE IS FRENCH FOR "BURNING CLOUD." IT'S A GLAMorous term for an incandescent event, the flaming, flying gas, ash, and lava fragments that burst from a volcano, often in its first stages of eruption. The nuée is typically only part of an eruption, bursting out of a vent that's been expanding, growing, ready to pop with heat and vapor, the harbinger and first part of a *pyroclastic flow*. That term literally means "fire fragments"—

pyro we all know, *clastic* meaning pieces. Every Earth Science student has seen and gasped at films of nuée ardentes in Geology 101, movies in which clouds of streaming gas flow down mountainsides like many-channeled rivers. They're bright orange and lightning fast. They leave nothing in their wake. Their speed and heat are the stuff of nightmares.

Nothing through the years has reminded me of those films so much as the time-lapse photos caught on wildlife cameras in Sonoma County parks and preserves during the October 8–9, 2017, firestorms. The cameras that recorded footage generally didn't survive the fires, but some of the data cards did. First, they caught the night, dark and tranquil. Then they picked up a whipping wind in the thrashing of trees and flying debris. Then, they logged photographs that grow brighter in succession, in which the wind is gusting—in a pressure system that generated tornadoes, it's been said—until, in the worst of it, hellacious infernos burst into the sky. Embers flew. Flame streamed like an orange tsunami, winds howled—a mix of gas, fire, and flying fragments that left nothing standing. It was a hint of apocalypse, climate change coming true. And it happened in a county of half a million people.

WE CBC BIRDERS HEAD FIRST FOR THE WILDWOOD VINEYARDS, our only stop of the day that didn't burn. The horizon is spiked with snags that were trees; hills and mountainsides are charcoal. Creekbeds once green with willow and blackberry are stripped bare. In Sonoma Valley, a third of all natural areas were charred. Down in Wildwood Vineyards, though, it's business as usual. Canada geese call and rise from misty ponds. Buffleheads and mallards raft over the mirrored water. Emerald grasses, hedges of dormant vines, clusters of redwood—all appear unchanged from last year.

Hopes lifting, we continue south. Maybe things won't be so bad. We go on to meet Trinity birder and ranch owner Julie

Atwood on her seventy-eight-acre property. Her vineyard and pasture on redwood-lined Calabazas Creek burned over twice, once on the first, terrifying night of the fire and then again in days that followed. "The fire started around ten at night and just missed our house," she says. "Embers were flying, the creek blazing, flames jumping through the canopy. Our forest smoldered and flared up for a month afterward." She looks at the woods, appraising them as though they've become something new and strange. "I still don't sleep at night."

We stroll the property, counting acorn woodpeckers, western bluebirds, white-crowned sparrows, and a surprising number of wrentits. Those latter birds have previously been in the higher elevations, among dry stands of chaparral. Here they are, though, skittering through Julie's garden down on the flats, not far from the creek.

The woods on the hills behind the ranch are scorched and smell of coal. Botanist Ann Howald, a twenty-five-year CBC birder, scans the blackened trees, certain that many are still alive. "The ponderosa pines are exceptionally well adapted to fire. Their thin, living layer can survive under that thick, charred bark depending on how hot it gets."

We split up to count both sides of Calabazas Creek, one of the main tributaries of Sonoma Creek. With the understory stripped out, streambanks are visible as we've never seen them. Previously impenetrable thickets are now heaps of ash. A pileated woodpecker pounding a limb is easy to spot through once-dense woods that are now blackened trunks and limbs. A Lincoln's sparrow forages stumps and singed logs that we never could have seen before the fire. The creek runs clear now, not impinged by ash, sparkling and shining among boulders and redwood logs.

We regroup near Julie's home, where we delight in our single rare bird of the day: a yellow-bellied sapsucker, perched like a holiday ornament on one of the only remaining persimmons.

~

"*SONOMA ES UN MANANTIAL A MANANTIALES*," WROTE FATHER José Altimira, when he first came to Sonoma Valley in 1823. "Sonoma is a fountain of fountains." Altimira's job: to found a mission in the Franciscan tradition of the Catholic faith. He'd come from Barcelona to work in the established mission in San Francisco but explored north when a new outpost was needed. Or wanted. It's been noted that the Northern California missions were part of a political strategy to help Spain head off Russian fur traders from colonizing further inland. Altimira's observation about Sonoma's oasis-like bounty meant that the water table was high and full, saturating soil, filling marshes, and overflowing streams. Altimira found the valley perfect for settling. In Sonoma, salmon (perhaps steelhead trout, perhaps Pacific salmon species) were plentiful. Ducks and geese filled the wetlands. Streams braided and flowed together, meeting in fresh- and brackish-water slough lands at the south end of the valley.

In the years following Altimira's arrival, and surely because of it, things changed. Mission San Francisco Solano lasted a mere eleven years, but its devastation to the area's ecology has rippled out for more than a century. The people who'd inhabited the land for millennia—Coast Miwok, Patwin, and Pomo family groups—were forced out of some thirty-five existing villages recorded in the mission census. They were the intended labor force, part of the Franciscan strategy. Enslaved, the Native Americans built, lived, and served the mission in what would become the City of Sonoma; mostly they died in astonishing numbers. Fifteen hundred baptisms in the mission's sterling history; nine hundred burials.

What was critical to the water narrative of Sonoma Valley was the abrupt change in lifestyle from indigenous to European. Without the original people stewarding the forested hills with small-fire burns, the practices that had aided the ecological health of the under- and overstory and had kept the hunting good for millennia stopped with unplanned suddenness. It's not a reach to say that, over the long haul, that lack of foresight in our European forebears contributed to the 2017 firestorm. Not to mention—though it speaks volumes—what colonization meant for the preexisting, complex cultures that could've taught the newcomers a thing or two hundred.

In place of the natural carrying capacity of the land and the indigenous people's constant vigilance of forests and fields, Europeans brought their cattle. A practice we imported with our bulls and cows, grazing imported beasts on the native-grass hills and valleys hit the land hard. Only natural ungulate roaming had preceded it. The effect of loading on thousands of hooved beasts that pretty much stayed where herded was like pressing a body with heavy stones. The soil in the landscape hardened as it does when packed down by the tires of all-terrain vehicles. Water continued to pour from natural springs up in headwaters areas, but now it encountered a changed, less permeable surface. It did what we all do when we hit smooth pavement. It sped up.

With the transformation of spongy soil to hardscape, Sonoma's creeks carved deeper channels into the landscape. That's the common response of streams to grazing and clearing, which we Europeans impressed on Western watersheds. The practices of longtime inhabitants had worked for millennia. Now streams incised deep, isolated beds that left forests high and dry above them.

It's dumbfounding to see these channels today. The few centuries of European influence have left lasting impacts—"legacy effects"—in their wake. With further development, and the continued installation of hardscape like asphalt, neighborhoods, industrial areas, and cement walkways, the creekbeds have responded by digging deeper. They're now fundamentally isolated flumes to the bay, unhooked from the surrounding uplands and no longer seasonally overflowing their banks into extensive wetlands.

The streams, bereft of much of their water through the same great transformation of the land, aren't the natural fire buffers and refuges they once were. On October 8, the first night of the Nuns Fire, thick riparian growth within and alongside dry channels helped funnel flames along their lengths. The town of Glen Ellen, which sits at the confluence of Calabazas Creek from the east and main Sonoma Creek from the north, and which is laced with numerous tributaries to both, coursed with fire that traveled along heavily wooded creekbeds as well as over the valley floor.

Historical drawings of Spanish *ranchos* established in the 1800s are embellished with ink squiggles representing streams running across and down the length of Sonoma Valley. The channels drawn by the mappers of the day are still here, but many of those lines no longer connect with the main stream. Instead they drop with insufficient flow beneath the gravels and cobbles in their beds, lost in alluvium. The creeks have always been seasonally dry in historic times, but still there's evidence in soil and vegetation that they're getting more so. Meadows that once boasted marshy soil are no longer fed by high underground water and creek overflow. Arid hillsides contain friable soil horizons resembling those in Utah and Arizona badlands. *Caliche*, rhyming with *peachy*, is a soil that geologists and paleontologists look for when charting ancient, arid soil horizons. Caliche results when heat and aridity wick moisture from deeper down in the soil, bringing water molecules up through the roots and branches of plants and by evaporation into the air. Caliche is a desert soil, until lately not generally associated with the moist, coastal hills of Northern California.

Tree-ring data in the stumps of logged trees, too, shows that conditions are getting drier. Biologists who study growth rings in downed oaks have observed increased gaps between rings from decades past. Such generous spacing can indicate bountiful, wet years of growth. Closer-spaced rings toward the bark are part of a record in wood of our climate growing drier and hotter.

Driving into the Mayacamas Mountains to find birds on fire-blackened slopes, we Christmas counters discover a "little green spot" among the overwhelmingly destroyed uplands. There, manzanita shrubs bloom with white, pendant flowers, and toyon bushes display bountiful, ripe berries. Anna's hummingbirds have honed in on them. The three-and-a-quarter-inch birds helicopter over the intact chaparral, buzzing and diving. It's an island of activity, drawing hummers from feeders on the valley floor, like every year. Otherwise, as David notes, the ridges are eerily quiet, "even if they didn't burn." There's a silence that sounds like the hush that follows great trauma.

At the mountaintop property of Trinity area birders Marc Schwager and Allison Ash, we hike among seared knobcone pine and other crispy chaparral. Allison tells us that she's noticed a curious absence of American robins. "They mobbed the hillside right after the fire," she says. "Now we're not seeing any." In the fading light, she points across the drainage to a denuded hillside. There, the Nuns Fire killed a neighbor in his home, "the one neighbor we lost."

As the Nuns Fire persisted for weeks, smoldering in some places, blowing up like napalmed jungle in others, the *whop-whop* of helicopters became a constant in Sonoma Valley. The tiny buckets of water they carried from farm ponds blew back on long, curving tethers, like afterthoughts. Ridiculously small. *They're fighting the fires with that?* But what else to do? Sonoma Valley doesn't have large reservoirs, as there aren't big rivers to dam. The crews had to get water where it lived, and in this valley, that's in small, private stores along perennial and intermittent streams. They had to lug it to steep, wooded hillsides dotted with multi-million-dollar homes.

"It was unimaginable," the Nuns Fire battalion chief and Sonoma Valley resident Bob Norrbom told fire professionals at a subsequent meeting. Three other fires, terrible conflagrations that had burned at previously unseen speeds into neighborhoods, were already raging nearby. All hands had been requested to fight those, and a fraction of what was needed responded. Stretched crews worked around the clock. In some instances, remote locations made communication impossible.

Phone service had been down since the beginning of the first blaze; evacuations had been initiated by word of mouth and through rushed, door-to-door notifications by both civilians and firefighters in the middle of the night. Some desperate residents, surrounded on all sides by flames, with all egress blocked, survived by submerging in their swimming pools.

The four combined fires that broke out in October 2017 are among twenty of the worst in one hundred years of North American records. They're known now as the Northern California Firestorm. Two-hundred-fifty fires across the state consumed 250,000 acres and 26,000 structures. Forty-six people died.

And the water? In Sonoma, it came by airship and by water tankers driven on remote roads and over long distances. The holding tanks of trucks were sometimes the only stores of water available at the site of a burning building. The CAL FIRE contractor from the state of Missouri who died fighting the Nuns Fire was driving one of those tankers on a curvy highway. Garrett Paiz, thirty-eight, crashed a guardrail when his truck's brakes gave out. He rolled into a heavily wooded ravine on the Napa side of the Mayacamas Mountains.

~

After dark, all nine Sonoma Valley CBC groups converge at the Sonoma Community Center for our traditional Count Dinner. The room is jovial, with three long tables full of birders enjoying local wine and chowder. Many come from the region's Madrone Audubon Society, including count founders Tom and Darren of Sonoma Birding-Sonoma Nature, a sponsor of the event.

Compiler Gene Hunn, also an Audubon member, runs down a list of species names; group leaders shout out a hearty "Yes!" if their group has seen the bird. As the numbers come in strong, a hum of excitement fills the room. "The total of 162 species is just above average for the previous twelve years [161.5 species]," Gene says, "and a shade short of last year's 164." While we counted fewer birds total—75 percent fewer individuals than in a typical year—the number of bird species remained high. Trinity birders tallied 71 species in our area, down a couple from last year but on par with our long-term average.

So the birds are still there, though a handful had shifted their locales. "Some species stand out as likely displaced by fires," Gene says. Band-tailed pigeons, which hide in dense habitat, were seen 350 percent more often than in a typical year. Their opaque roosting areas had simply burned away. In the Trinity area, wrentits—usually found in chaparral sites—were seen not far from the numerous band-tailed pigeons near the valley floor. American robins, by contrast, were not only scarce from their usual haunts, they were also counted at just over twenty percent of average. California thrashers, associated with the upland chaparral, weren't spotted in the Trinity at all. David says he's seen similar redistributions of species before, even without record fires. "Especially in wet or dry years, birds spread out or group up around water," he says. "Today they're in the unburned areas. They find someplace to be."

It's an oasis-like effect, a coming together where habitat is hospitable in an overwhelmingly denuded and charred landscape. Birds congregate at the rush-edged ponds, or in the one green patch of chaparral, or in Julie's streamside garden.

It's a hopeful night after the count, "a community moment and pretty powerful," as David says. Seeing the presence of life where we'd expected none is both encouraging and instructive. As Trinity birder Christine Engle says, "In dynamic California, with its fires, earthquakes, and floods, the birds teach us about beauty and survival." To which I add: the water we all depend upon teaches us about ourselves.

15.

THE OASIS THIS TIME

W HEN I WAS A YOUNG GIRL EXPLORING THE DESERTS of California and Arizona with my family, I learned about dry camping. Each night we had a finite amount of water that we had carried in by car or backpacks, limited stores not to be wasted by spilling or overuse. We'd be anywhere and nowhere—a roadside rest stop, a national monument campground, a small-town park consisting of acres of struggling lawn and two forlorn picnic tables. In those moments, guided by my mother and father, I learned to make a little go a long way. The value of water imprinted on my cells as we meted out portions of the precious resource. Using only what was needed taught me respect for and connection to water that I hadn't known simply from turning on a tap.

As a Colorado River guide in my twenties and thirties, I felt the power of water from rowing heavy boats in big whitewater. A reversal of flow could buck people from their seats—strong men and women, who'd been holding on tight one moment and lost their grips the next. A deep, hidden current could grab the oars from my hands as if I had no more strength than an infant. At other times, I let the river take me just where I wanted to go. In those moments, the water became my biggest ally.

As a fluvial (stream) geologist, I puzzled over the traces of water in modern and ancient environments. Jumbled bones in river sandstones, from the carcasses of now-extinct creatures that came to rest where rivers carried them in flood. The power of water, what it gives as well as takes away, is evident once it's gone.

Today, as then, we live and die with and by water.

Taken to extremes, poor water husbandry destabilizes cultures. The Middle Eastern refugee crisis that hit new heights in the mid 2010s stemmed from water instability driven by water mismanagement and a changing climate. In 2014, the United Nations reported that an estimated eight hundred thousand people lost their livelihoods due to water deprivation in the Middle East. "Water scarcity is forcing people off the land," said Hussein Amery, a water management expert at the Colorado School of Mines, in a 2015 interview with National Public Radio. "These refugees are very much water refugees."

In the American West, much of the drawing down of water stores relates to creating the faux oasis, the Cadillac Desert identified in 1986 by author and water-resources consultant Marc Reisner. "In the West, it is said, water flows uphill toward money. And it literally does, as it leaps three thousand feet across the Tehachapi Mountains in gigantic siphons to slake the thirst of Los Angeles, as it is shoved a thousand feet out of Colorado River canyons to water Phoenix and Palm Springs and the irrigated lands around them."

Even back when Reisner wrote his seminal book, it was the eleventh hour at the oasis—11:59 p.m., in truth—past time to act. Certainly the responsibility lies with us all.

Our desire for oasis will never leave us. It's as tied to our DNA as family, community, and a good story. To help the natural oasis to endure, though, we'll have to ease our obsession with the faux oasis. The palm-studded sanctuary will always grip our imaginations. The more we foster it in the wild or create green systems for water treatment and recycling in urban settings, the more we protect our wild rivers, lakes, and springs. That is the fix.

~

ALL RIGHT, THEN, HERE ARE SOME GESTURES, SOME THAT MAY matter only to ourselves.

I can drink and use fresh water with mindfulness. I can give it my deepest respect. The Buddhists teach us to Do No Harm. I do no harm to other creatures by intentionally conserving water that they need, too.

I can open to the idea that water conservation is likely the new normal. Where does leadership begin? Why not with me, with the smallest, most mindful actions? I can integrate thoughtful use as a way of life. I can choose not to plant water-intensive trees and shrubs.

I can work within my community. I can support the building of infrastructure for recycled water. I can support legislation that requires water-saving devices in all homes and businesses.

I can help protect water sources for wildlife in the parks and forests near me. I can follow the rules that are there to respect water source areas, important to public health and safety.

I know the river that slakes my thirst. In the Northern California town I called home for decades, drinking water is piped south from the Russian River to the north, which draws from the Eel River even farther away. A swim in the Eel or a walk beside its banks is a journey into knowing what is at stake if we drain it. When I learn where my water comes from, everything changes. I act with new awareness. If I have a choice between my green lawn or a water-fed wild place my children and grandchildren can enjoy, I know which I would choose.

I'd choose the world in which we shelter the natural oasis that has long sheltered us.

ACKNOWLEDGMENTS

A GRATEFUL THANK YOU TO THE MANY GENEROUS INDIVIDUALS and organizations who've supported this work about water and oases in the North American West. Supreme appreciation to Fulbright Canada and the US Fulbright Programs for the award of a 2014/15 Visiting Research Chair at the University of Alberta, Edmonton, and the opportunity to research water issues north of the forty-ninth parallel. The Council for the International Exchange of Scholars in Washington, D.C., provided critical help, as did the entire Fulbright Canada team. I'm deeply in debt to those who shared their expertise in Alberta and British Columbia, especially Suzanne Bayley, Katharine Binhammer, Ted Bishop, Albert Braz, Chris Chang Yen Phillips, Dianne Chisholm, Curtis Clarke, Lois Harder, Jane Heather, Katherine Koller, Leslea Kroll, Sarah Krotz, Bob Longworth, Hannah McGregor, Colleen Murphy, Michael O'Driscoll, Lahoucine Ougazine, Lyana Patrick, David Schindler, Conrad Scott, Mark Simpson, Peter Sinnema, Tom Wharton, Janice Williamson, Sheena Wilson, Rita Wong, and Heather Zwicker. Any misrepresentation of the scholarship they shared is on me.

Special thanks to Janet MacDonald and Kelly Sendall of the Royal British Columbia Museum for arranging the original invitation to conduct research in the city of Victoria. I'm indebted as well to those in my Fulbright Canada cohort, especially Ann Chen, Christopher Lupke, Margaret Moss, and Alan Wallis, for their friendship and insight.

In Sonoma County, geographer Arthur Dawson, educator Jessica Glatt, author Julia Whitty, and hydrologist David Leland supported my research plan and read drafts of some of the chapters. My longtime river friend Teal Kinnamun assisted from Mexico. Some of my closest literary friends in the States reviewed early pages of this book: Debra Gwartney, Sarah Rabkin, Kathryn Wilder, and Andy Weinberger, to name a few.

The Island Institute in Sitka, Alaska, contributed significantly to my work through the gift of a 2011 writing residency. Many thanks to former co-directors Carolyn Servid and Dorik Mechau and my hosts David and Marge Steward for the time they afforded me on Thimbleberry Bay. Thanks as well to Jim Dice and Elaine Tulving of the Steele/Burnand Anza-Borrego Desert Research Center in Borrego Springs, California, where I wrote the proposal that won the Waterston Desert Writing Prize and evolved into this book. Ellie Waterston and the Desert Writing Prize team graced me with their support and an introduction to PLAYA in Summer Lake, Oregon, where I drafted some of these chapters. A special nod to Deb Ford and John Martin of PLAYA for their friendship and gifts of time and space for deep writing. I'm deeply appreciative of Marla Hastings and Dave Boyd of Occidental, California, J. J. Baugher of Seattle, and Mark Christopulos and Jen Slajus formerly of Ann Arbor, Michigan, who offered their homes for writing and research time. They also offered important ideas that permeate this book's chapters.

My siblings, Timothy, Jennifer, and Jonathan Lawton, are my longtime partners in exploring nature, having grown up close to the astounding outdoors shared with us by our parents, Russell and Mary Lawton. We took countless, amazing trips around and out of the Pacific Northwest where our family has roots. I still live with the Columbia River in my blood, as well as with the deserts, rivers, and lakes of our youths.

My profoundest thanks to Kirsten Johanna Allen, Mark Bailey, Anne Terashima, Rachel Davis, and the rest of the superlative team at Torrey House Press. We'd planned to work together on a book of fiction many years ago. Those plans changed, but Torrey House later backed this book with their customary passion. There is no way I would have written it without their support. May they win accolades, prizes, the universe's best karma, and the realization of their mission— beyond their wildest dreams—of promoting environmental conservation through literature. The world needs their work.

Finally, deep gratitude to my husband, Paul Christopulos, who puts all his heart and soul into our life together, and to my daughter, Rose McMackin, for her precious friendship, trust, and exceptional insight. To Paul and Rose, my love forever.

About the Author

Rebecca Lawton is a Western author, fluvial geologist, and former Colorado River guide. Her books about water and river subcultures include *Reading Water: Lessons from the River* (*San Francisco Chronicle* Bay Area Bestseller and ForeWord Nature Book of the Year Finalist). Her pieces for general audiences have been published in *Aeon, Audubon, Brevity, Hakai, Orion, Shenandoah, Sierra, Undark*, and many other journals. Her creative writing honors include a 2014/15 Fulbright Scholarship, the 2006 (inaugural) Ellen Meloy Fund Award for Desert Writers, the 2015 (inaugural) Waterston Desert Writing Prize, a 2014 WILLA award for original softcover fiction, Pushcart Prize nominations in fiction, nonfiction, and poetry, and residencies at Hedgebrook Retreat for Women Writers, The Island Institute, and PLAYA. She lives at the Cascade Mountain-Great Basin interface in Summer Lake, Oregon, where she directs PLAYA's residency program for artists, writers, and scientists.